Dogmatic Slumber

My Journey to Awakening

David Mackaman

© 2014 David Mackaman
ISBN-13: 978-1499540116
ISBN-10: 1499540116
Cover photo: Pilgrim station at Glendalough

Author's Note

I am not a historian. This is my story based upon a series of events and anecdotes that, to the best of my recollection, are true and accurate. If I got something wrong—a timeline, a detail—I'm sorry about that. Please forgive me. I have endeavored to relay my impression of these events and the impact that they had on me as honestly and purely as I could. That aspect of the story is the most important thing and is resolute.

I have fond thoughts about every person included in this story. If by chance I have offended anybody, please let me know so that I can apologize. No offense was intended.

To Doug and Henry

"I must, therefore, abolish knowledge, to make room for belief. The dogmatism of metaphysics, that is, the presumption that it is possible to advance in metaphysics without previous criticism, is the true source of the unbelief (always dogmatic) which militates against morality."

~Immanuel Kant (Second Edition Preface to *The Critique of Pure Reason*)

Chapter 1
Takeoff

As I looked out over the plane's wing, I imagined a shadowy figure, a gremlin clawing away at the jet engine. Red and green sparks flew as he scratched and tore the plane's metallic skin. He jumped up and down, snarling menacingly at the sky, then turned his furious glare towards me. His blazing red eyes, demonic and filled with bad intent, locked onto mine. He pointed and mouthed the words through his wretched sharp teeth: "You're going down in flames! You know who I am!"

And it was true. I did know who he was—probably the same gremlin that had penetrated my consciousness several months ago, twisted my thoughts, and sabotaged my sorry, middle-aged life. Actually, my life hadn't been that sorry up until now. But he was right. I probably was going down in flames.

"You'll be sorry." The imp cackled as he jumped off the plane's wing, a handful of loose wires dangling to the ground. Probably right about that too, I thought. He smiled then disappeared.

I closed my mind to the image of the gremlin and turned my head inward to the dimly lit cabin. I breathed out and then in, more in than out. The cabin air was stuffy; my hands were clammy. I fidgeted purposelessly. I reached out for my left knee, then my right knee. I crossed my arms, leaned back and rocked forward. I reached behind my head, grabbed my neck and ran my hands through my hair, first up the back of my head and then from the front to the back to smooth my hair.

I folded both arms back across my chest then raised my right hand to wipe the window to no avail. It was still dark outside and my effort to clear the mercurial condensation on the glass was futile. The view from my window seat was dark and murky. I couldn't see where I was going. Appropriate.

Everything in my life had built or perhaps disassembled to this. The sense of exhilaration I was trying to feel was smothered by uncertainty. What have I done? What was I doing? While I wished to resolve these questions in my mind and move on, I could not. I settled into the posture that the proper response to these questions was doubt. Not clarity, but ambiguity. Not confidence, but uncertainty. Not excitement, but a sickening foreboding that I was lost and heading into unchartered waters. My probable road to misery was paved with rash decisions. Had I really thought this thing through? Nope.

The expensive car lease, the plane tickets, the rental home in the Loire Valley, retiring—no, vacating my career forever. Could I afford any of this? Should I be doing this? Why on earth? Was this insane? Wasn't this insane??? These thoughts and more positive, constructive thoughts had been doing battle in my head for the past year as I pondered, ultimately decided, and began going through the act of retiring at age 55.

As the moment of departure approached, the dark, negative, doubtful thoughts were trouncing their opponent. No one does this. I was haunted by doubt and guilt. Guilt! I wouldn't be working any more, and probably never would again. That's not like me! I had always worked harder than others, always done more than my share. My wife, Laura, had been supportive, if not completely understanding. She was staying home, saddled into her nursing career that she loves. Me? I was traipsing off to Europe for the better part of four months with no plan beyond that. Guilt—yes, guilt separated by intermittent moments of panic.

No! Turn back! Don't do this! Too late.

I closed my eyes and rubbed my forehead with the first three fingers of my right hand, using my thumb to massage my temple. I ran my hand down my face and neck, sighed, and looked over at my son, Will, sitting in the aisle seat next to me. No surprise. His head was back, his mouth open, and his eyes closed. He was sleeping soundly in the pre-dawn darkness.

Our route would take us from Des Moines, to Chicago, to London, and to Amsterdam. Upon arrival in Amsterdam we were to pick up the Renault, my rental car for the next several months, and drive to Groningen in the Netherlands near the North Sea. Will would stay at Groningen, studying spatial science for spring semester. I would drive from Groningen to France, where I would join up with a group of American college students also studying abroad. These students were with a foreign study program based in the small French village of Pontlevoy. This program was organized by my cousin, Doug, who had invited me to help out this coming semester

As our plane pulled away from the gate, more dark thoughts crept into my head. Will is smart and athletic, but a quiet person. He'd travelled to Europe, Mexico, and across the U.S., but never on his own. Would he be able to find his way along? Would he be able to make friends in the Netherlands? Would he be able to adapt to the culture and the foreign learning environment? The curriculum at the University of Groningen, a historic institution founded over 400 years ago, was reputedly tough. Grades are awarded on a scale of 1-10, and 10s were never awarded. Room? Board? Grades? Would his phone work? Could he get in touch if he had a problem? Had we (by that, I mean *I*) overrepresented his skill level to the soccer club he hoped to train with? Through email on Will's behalf, I represented that he was at the highest level of amateur play in the U.S. That puts him on the first or second tiers of this club. Had I overrepresented his skill? Hell no! Maybe. Probably. Doubt. Doubt. Doubt.

As the plane continued its taxi, I thought about my story, the cause and effects that brought me to seat 11A on this plane. I was a former banker, a recently retired bank president for Wells Fargo in Des Moines. I was an English major in college at the University of Iowa. The truth is that I never intended to be a banker and probably never should have been one. It was an accident, one that, for better or worse, was my life's course for more than 30 years. It was neither all bad nor all good.

The good was that I was able to gain personal reward through a few significant aspects of my career.

For instance, I did like teaching, coaching, and mentoring young people—not about banking so much, but about life skills such as communication, leadership, ethical behaviors, and being of service to others. A big part of mentoring for me was both being self-aware and creating self-awareness for others. It is critical for one to be aware of one's individual strengths and talents and to build upon those things. Likewise, it is important for one to be aware of weaknesses and blind spots in order to develop strategies to work around those things. I always found coaching and mentoring around self-awareness and personal development to be highly rewarding.

I also loved the community aspect of being a bank president: launching and supporting initiatives that made the world a more interesting place, helping lift up and support those in need, creating excitement in others about the beauty of diverse ethnic personalities and cultures. Deep down the need for me to leave the world a better place than I found it, a better place for my being, has always been core to my sense of self and purpose.

In addition, I loved the leadership part of my career, which I always associated with visioning and storytelling. The art of crafting and articulating a vision for the future, a story told in such a compelling way that others would get excited and want to be a part of it, was perhaps the thing that I loved above everything else about my work.

All that said, despite the fact that my career allowed me to teach, that I was able to impact the community, and that I was able to hone my leadership talents through the art of storytelling, I was still on balance not well-suited to enjoy many of the responsibilities of my job. I was an English major, for crying out loud. I voted democratic. I cared for the underdog, for the 99% that marched into to the bank's lobby to demonstrate fervently. I didn't belong to the conservative business realm of banking. In many ways I was an imposter who hid my true self beneath the veneer of my own skin.

I have nothing against the company I worked for, Wells Fargo. In fact I believe Wells Fargo to be the best bank in the world. Wells is a high-performing organization with a clearly defined sense of ethics and values. That said, the company's fixation on growth and performance is endemic of the culture that exists in general for all of corporate America. The stock market rewards companies that win the war for market share and punishes those who lose the war. Wells Fargo just happens to be one of the most consistent victors, and for good reason. Wells is obsessed with the discipline of financial performance and revenue growth.

Being a bank president at Wells Fargo, to me, represented a seemingly endless string of days wrought with stress and tension that worked together to painfully tighten my neck and shoulder muscles and to stifle the flows of joy and creativity.

I found myself in an unnatural world where every single tomorrow had to be better than today, every day a new record. The vantage point you'd worked so hard to gain, wherever you stood today was not good enough. Something more, something different, something "better" was always needed, the true definition of discontent and unhappiness.

At Wells Fargo, goals were specific, measurable, and intensely managed, continually ratcheted up each year, each month, each week, each day—yesterday's result, forgotten; tomorrow's numbers, your burden to deliver. Every conceivable outcome—product sales, loan production, compliance errors, whether the tellers smiled or not, you name it—was stack-ranked across the entire company. By virtue of these rankings, one's performance was constantly compared, measured, and assessed. And, by virtue of these rankings, one's worth was established. This incessant stack-ranking of human performance was, to me, inhuman and something that never felt good regardless of whether I was ranked towards the top, the middle, or the bottom of the class.

The environment was very competitive, at times ruthlessly so. Managers were constantly asked to identify their lower two decile sales performers and to develop plans of how they intended to "help" these individuals move up, or out, and within what timelines. My calendar was hectic, almost always fully booked, overflowing with back-to-back appointments all day long, every day. I was always in a rush, a tendency that spilled over and spoiled many aspects of my personal life.

It seemed as though only problems walked through my office door, that the phone only rang with difficulties to confront. During a typical day I would often be in meetings for hours on end, many of them over the phone. Reading loan applications, complying with detailed and unnecessary banking regulations was, for me, tedious and soul-sapping. And then there were the constant reorganizations, realignments, and downsizings. Always, always, always being asked to do more with less and delivering dispassionate bad news to people you cared about. "Your position has been eliminated. It's a business decision."

So, while I enjoyed some aspects of my career, on balance the core elements repulsed me and over time wore me down. With this orientation, I decided to vacate my career as early as I could, which at Wells Fargo is 55 years old, the magic day stock options become fully vested. My career had certainly been a means to establish a viable nest egg—no complaints. But I never really wanted to be a banker. The thought of being one for the remainder of my days when I still had the health and energy to try something new was deplorable. Thus, I told my boss a year in advance of my 55th birthday that I planned to retire on or about the

8th of January, 2013. To his credit, he kept this information confidential and could not have been more supportive during the year leading up to my retirement.

During the fall of 2012, I made my retirement decision public. I had to explain to people why I was doing this and what I planned to do next. My "why" followed along the lines that I simply wanted to do something else with the rest of my life, something other than what I was currently doing or what I had already done. My "what next" response involved writing more (perhaps a book), exploring spiritual aspects of the human condition that I had to this point in my life deferred, working to be more physically healthy through more consistent exercise and better diet, and perhaps teaching. Who knew? Maybe someday I'd end up working for a non-profit to help make the world a better place, maybe an environmental cause. Despite the fact that my "what next" spiel sounded like typical midlife crisis drivel, the possibility of a new life was essential to me.

My first post-retirement gig was to travel to Pontlevoy, France. My cousin, Doug, is a French History professor on staff at the University of Southern Mississippi in Hattiesburg. Doug actually lives in St. Paul and coordinates foreign studies through programs sponsored by the USM. One of Doug's programs is the Abbey Program at Pontlevoy, where American college students go to study abroad for a semester. The Abbey itself is a nearly 1,000-year-old cathedral and monastery. Pontlevoy is a small village situated on the plateau between the Loire and the Cher Rivers, maybe a two-hour train ride south of Paris. My destined role at the Abbey Program was to provide informal lectures around core leadership talents such as visioning, ethics, active listening skills, etc.

Sounds groovy, eh? No. Sounds irresponsible and ill-conceived.

I snapped back to the present moment, sitting in 11A. Doubts and anxiety permeated my being. I sighed, took a deep breath, and exhaled with my eyes closed as the jet engines roared. The plane accelerated down the dark, wet runway and began to separate from the ground. We were off. I was no longer contemplating the thought of jumping off a cliff. I had jumped. The thought of going back, while still racing in my mind, was impossible.

Chapter 2
Who Am I?

So who am I?

My name is David Mackaman. I was raised in Des Moines, Iowa, the youngest child and only son of Wayne and Edith Mackaman, both deceased. I have three older sisters: Sarah, Ruth, and Julie are thirteen, ten, and seven years older than me, respectively. All three of them are successful, settled, happy, and delightful.

Sarah lives on Whidbey Island, north of Seattle with her partner, Dick. Sarah is brilliant, always factually correct, well-rationalized, and well-researched. She is also sentimental and nostalgic, both good traits. She remembers and sees things fondly, perhaps better than they actually were or are. Sarah retired as a highly compensated logistics consultant for IBM.

Ruth is a diminutive dynamo who lives on the upper east side of Manhattan on 5th Avenue with her husband, Jim. Ruth retired as a foreign exchange consultant for Brown Brothers Herriman on Wall Street and is now a whole-hearted devotee to healthiness. She is a vegetarian and a yoga practitioner, holding the equivalent of a black belt in that arena.

Julie spent most of her career in San Francisco working as a grant writer. In this capacity she became an expert consultant for independent film makers. Julie and her husband, Rick, have retired to a country home in Vermont. Julie gushes life, enthusiasm, and energy in ways that have to be seen to be believed. Julie is always on, literally in your face with zeal and zest.

I love all of my sisters, and yet we are so different. In a sense we are like the four seasons. Julie is spring, eternally blooming and colorful. Ruth is summer, warm and comfortable. Sarah has the wisdom and sentimentality of autumn. I was born on a cold clear winter day in January. All of us have set off in different directions. And for whatever reason, I'm the one that stayed closest to home. I'm the one who built a life and career in our hometown, Des Moines.

Des Moines, at least in my mind while I was growing up, was a dreary, uninspiring, gray town. In retrospect, it was a good place—wholesome and healthy, centered around goodness, community, family, and neighbors. It was not a particularly exciting or stimulating place. I never had any intention of remaining in Des Moines once I was grown. But for a variety of reasons, this has been my home as an adult. I have zero regret. Des

Moines has burgeoned over the years and exploded with diverse cultural vitality. With a metro population of around 600,000, Des Moines is of a distinctive and rare size. The city has been able to stave off the dehumanizing aspects of a larger metropolis. And yet Des Moines has been able to blend the best aspects of a peaceful life with the excitement of a bohemian culture. In Des Moines, those two extremes flourish hand in hand.

I have been able to build a long and strong network of diverse personal relationships and friendships in Des Moines. I have had the joy of being able to make a personal impact on the community through engaging with various civic and non-profit organizations. It is important to me that my life and my actions make a difference for others, not just today, but far into the future. Des Moines is my home and it has been a great pleasure over the last 30 years or so to be part of, and in some instances lead, the transformation that has happened there.

Accordingly, my life in Des Moines has in most ways been really great, the aforementioned downside tradeoffs to my career choice aside. Laura Lautenbach, one of Des Moines's beautiful natives, agreed to my marriage proposal after three years of dating. We met at the University of Iowa, where Laura earned a nursing degree and I received an English degree and an MBA. We were 22 years old when we married, which now seems an incredibly imprudent young age. But we've beaten the odds and forged a life together for which I am oh so grateful.

Laura is a Registered Nurse, a fantastic one, who works with cardiac patients on an outpatient basis. She is wonderful and caring. She cannot resist her calling, which is to help those in need, whether that means caring for and healing patients, helping out with an afterschool art of reading program, or delivering meals to local homeless shelters. Laura is most concerned with those in need and with those that are disadvantaged.

For many years, Laura served as team manager for Will's soccer teams. This was not a typical soccer mom gig. Will's teams were a potpourri of immigrant boys and young men from faraway places such as Sudan, Ivory Coast, Sierra Leone, Bosnia, Mexico, and El Salvador. Being team manager included assisting with payment of club dues, shuttling players to and from practices and matches, paying for hotel accommodations, driving carloads of players to cities throughout the Midwest, preparing team meals, and providing encouragement, support, and advice to the boys as well as to their parents. As a result, many of these young men were able to use the game of soccer as a means to gain a toehold in America, and ultimately as a way to access and pay for a college education, something that was otherwise unthinkable.

Laura, of Dutch heritage, is, if nothing else, committed to cleanliness. Our funky, mid-century house is clean, our yard is tidy, our laundry machine is constantly in motion, and our neighborhood is free of litter thanks to Laura's daily walks with our dog, Maya. These walks always begin with an empty litter bag, which is full by walk's end.

Laura and I have two grown children. Audrey lives on Whidbey Island, Washington and is an independent copyeditor and budding author. Will is a college student at Macalester College in St Paul.

I always wonder with skepticism how people can sincerely describe their spouse as their "soul mate." Laura and I have a wonderful life-long love affair, and yet we are in so many ways different and independent from one another. Laura is kind, gentle, and polite. I, on the other hand, have a well-deserved reputation of being brutally honest and direct. Laura doesn't like to make waves. I like to startle people, to grab their attention by asking them to consider a provocative perspective. Laura attends a Lutheran Church and is buoyed by her faith. I do not and am not. I love to read and express myself verbally. Laura prefers movies. I love to travel, experience adventure, risk, and explore the unknown. We have a family saying that "Laura wouldn't like that" which applies to things such as adventure, risk, and the exploring the unknown.

(The saying originated during a family sailing expedition through the inside passage of Alaska. Laura has a seasick tendency and declined the trip. The trip was great, but included a near-death experience. Our boat's engines faltered and we were nearly dashed on the rocks of the icy Frederick Sound. Windswept swells tossed our powerless boat as we bobbed up and down with the icebergs. A shoreline of jagged rocks approached, looming as our inevitable destiny. During the darkest moments of the experience, someone quipped, "Well, Laura wouldn't like this!" As good fortune would have it, the ship's anchors grabbed purchase just a few short feet from disaster and a salmon fishing boat ultimately came along to tow us to safety. But the saying that "Laura wouldn't have liked that" has stuck to Laura, unwanted like a wet dog at a party, despite the fact that she had nothing to do with the incident and despite the fact that none of us liked that incident.)

Unlike Laura, I have this unwavering need to do something else, a dissatisfaction with what I'm currently doing, a need to see what's around the corner that's different and possibly—no probably—better than what's here and now. I go fishing in remote, adventuresome regions of the Arctic Circle, Saskatchewan, and Ontario—not Laura. I travel with Will to soccer's World Cup in South Africa, venturing into wild places and Johannesburg's settlements where white men "should not go"—not Laura. I camp and raft down the powerful and unpredictable rapids of the Grand Canyon—not Laura. I backpack in the snow-packed Sierra Mountains or New Mexico's arid Gila Wilderness—not Laura. I venture to the fjords and glacier bays of Alaska—not Laura. I ran a marathon—not Laura. I bike, play tennis, and golf—not Laura.

I quit my job and head off to Europe for the better part of four months to find myself—not Laura. Laura loves what she's doing. She has no need to change or enhance her life with more excitement. I do. I am restless. She is not. But regardless of our differences, the biggest part of who I am is Laura's husband and Audrey and Will's father. I love them all dearly.

That said, it is my parents, Edith and Wayne Mackaman, who were the architects of my foundation.

Edith was an only child raised by her father. Her mother died of the Spanish Flu during childbirth. Edith was a petite woman, extremely well-read. She skipped two levels of grade school and graduated from Drake University in Des Moines. Throughout her life, my mother would go to the Franklin Avenue Library weekly, if not more frequently, to return a stack of five to six books she and my father had finished reading. Upon returning with last week's books, she would then select a heavy armload of new books for the upcoming week. Edith was leader of her Great Books Reading Club and read every great book, several times. (I remember once when I was an adolescent. I walked by Edith as she was reading on the couch and noticed that she was reading Einstein's Theory of Relativity. Say what, Ma?)

Edith was sweet, polite, and kind, if not terribly demonstrative of love and affection. I attribute the latter quality to her upbringing as an only child reared by her father who must have been both decimated by his wife's death during childbirth and completely unaware of how to raise their daughter on his own.

My mother was a very, very nice woman, very bright, and a wonderful mother. She never had a cross or unkind word for anyone. She didn't care for conflict, aggression, or disagreements other than those involving civil and respectful discussions. Edith was optimistic. She had a lifelong saying: "Well, if that's the worst thing that ever happens to you..." She dug this saying out whenever something terrible happened. Her point—

that you could either remember or imagine something worse happening—was her ineffective way of reinforcing a positive outlook in her children.

Edith was a homemaker back in the day when that was the common lot for most women. She did at one time work in the bookkeeping department at Bankers Life (n/k/a The Principal Group) in downtown Des Moines while Wayne fought in World War II. However, when Wayne returned from the war, she left the workforce and began immediately raising her family. The term "immediate" is the appropriate word choice. My oldest sister, Sarah, was born nine months and one day from Wayne's return from the war.

Politically very liberal, my mother was enthralled by the Iowa Caucus and Democratic Convention. She followed both processes diligently for hours on end and was always well-informed politically. Edith volunteered at the polls, was a two-gallon blood donor, and periodically filled in when the Drake University switchboard was short staffed.

The entire world, or at least the part that knew her, saw Edith as a gem, which is what she was. She was never sick, not particularly physically active, but healthy her entire life up until she was diagnosed with cancer at age 78. A tumor in her heart quickly metastasized and killed her within a month of its discovery. Edith died a very kind, considerate, generous, well-educated, well-read, and thoughtfully rationalized atheist.

My father, Wayne, came from a large family compared to my mother's single-child, single-parent upbringing. My father's parents, Frank and Eva

Mackaman, represented fine Midwestern stock, both coming from small, rural Iowa settings. Frank was an attorney and in many respects, both professionally and personally, a pioneer. Eva was a schoolteacher in small-town Iowa before marrying Frank and moving to Des Moines. Both graduated from Drake University, as ultimately would all of their children.

My grandmother, Eva, was such a nice person—wholesome, nice, gentle, very maternal and grandmotherly. She was wonderful and she was, in all aspects that I was aware, pure. She was a regular church-goer who never drank, never swore, and was never cross. She never learned to drive a car, though she could ride a horse and drive a buggy. It is not possible for me to imagine Eva angry or upset. She was even-keeled and quietly, but positively, charged. I remember so fondly the nights I would spend at her apartment, just her and I, playing a card game she taught me called Muggins. We would bake cookies and cornbread. I would check books out from the library and we would read them together. She would take me fishing for crappies at our family cabin in Minnesota, walk me to the orchard to pick apples for homemade applesauce and pies, and later write regular letters to me when I went away to college. Like no one else, Eva made my young self feel loved and important. And I loved her in return.

My grandfather, Frank, died before I was born. I never knew him. But by reputation his personality contrasted starkly with my grandmother's. Eva was kind and meek. Frank was smart, strong-willed, independent, and acerbic. He had the capacity to charm young children, but his love was tough. His temper was often quick. His politics were conservative, his tolerance for poor judgments was low, and his punishment could be abrupt and severe. He was busy and capable, a true Renaissance man, a master of all trades.

Throughout Frank's life, he never forgot his rural roots and always maintained a hobby farm, which included a garden and a sparse collection of horses, chickens, and maybe a cow or two, but never a goat. He had a saying that he passed on to his children and they onto me: "Remember, you can always buy a goat, but you can never sell one." I have applied that parcel of wisdom, never with respect to goats, but with respect to other similar things on several occasions during my life.

Besides practicing law, Frank was involved in the founding of several businesses and organizations in Des Moines including the Des Moines Savings and Loan, the Portland Cement Company, and the Des Moines Golf and Country Club (n/k/a Waveland Golf Course). To my knowledge, he never played golf and was not motivated by money.

The Great Depression took its toll, and Frank did not leave behind a very substantial estate, except for two remarkable parcels of real estate, two places that have, over the years, provided unimaginable and enduring importance and value to me and my entire family.

Cedar Lake, Minnesota

In 1915 Frank and Eva bought an island on Cedar Lake near Aitkin, Minnesota. They bought the property from Frank's half-brother, Will Mackaman (my son's namesake) for $100.00. The property deed to Will Mackaman was signed by Theodore Roosevelt. Frank hand-built a cabin on the island and forged a causeway made of dirt and rock that connected the island to the mainland. The original cabin was built without electricity or plumbing. It was razed during 1985 to make way for a new, more habitable structure.

This place at Cedar Lake, a place we call MacIsland, has become a monumental gathering point for the Mackaman clan. We return to this place each summer in family clusters, as we have for nearly 100 years. The extended Mackaman family is scattered across the country, but this place on Cedar Lake has held us together. It remains our common bond. Here is where our lives overlap. This is where we celebrate and renew our love for each other. This is where we admire nature together—the herons, eagles, and loons, sunrises and sunsets, stars, and northern lights, the fresh breezes, and the sweet smell of pine. This is where we dive from the dock into the deep, cool waters. This is where we swim, sail, kayak, and fish. This is where we bike, play cards, read, nap, play, and listen to music. This is where we gather for home-cooked meals, where we talk, laugh, tell stories, and sometimes cry.

> We have all been tremendously affected by my grandfather's foresight to build this legacy place, this priceless heirloom that has come to serve as glue for generation after generation.

The Farm

Prior to World War II, Frank and Eva purchased 80 acres of timber ground a few miles north of Des Moines. They built a log cabin in the woods and later a home named "Springview." This place became known as "the Farm." The log cabin in particular was an amazing homage to Americana, with its fieldstone fireplace, grand picnic tables to accommodate large family gatherings, Aladdin oil lamps for light, a loft with a bed, and the old Victrola record player in the bedroom. Over the years we would hold many family reunions at the Farm, celebrate holidays there, ice skate on the farm's pond, picnic at the cabin, and ride horses. My parents would often drop me and my friends off at the Farm. We would spend the entire day there exploring, climbing trees, building forts, and hunting for frogs, snakes, or morel mushrooms.

The Farm was sold and the money divided some years ago. However, I will always be keenly aware of the adventuresome spirit and love of nature that developed in me there.

Together, Frank and Eva raised six children: five boys, including my father, and one girl. These were my aunt and uncles, people who would become my absolute role models in life. All of them, my aunt and uncles, were smart, honest, hardworking, successful, caring, witty, and well-read storytellers. I aspire that someday these same words can be used to describe me. To receive a compliment or to have an achievement noticed by an aunt or an uncle was to me the equivalent of an Olympic gold medal.

Sadly, these individuals are all dead now. But I continue to look up to them. These were remarkable people. I have done all that I possibly could to emulate them. There are 17 cousin descendants from Frank and Eva, 16 living including me and my three sisters. My cousins represent the most diverse group of fantastic people that can be imagined. These individuals, my cousins and my sisters, are all truly brothers and sisters to me.

And while it is true that my aunts and uncles were unbelievably inspirational to me, my father, Wayne, was different from the rest. The third oldest of six, Wayne was darker, not as joyful, and far less outgoing and positive than the rest of his family. There was unspoken knowledge in the family that Wayne's World War II experience had been very difficult and contributed to his emotional moodiness and sometimes darkness.

During WWII, Wayne was captain of a landing craft in Italy, North Africa, and Normandy. I remember once as a young boy when my older cousin Charlie, who at the time lived just up the street, confided in me. His parents had warned him that if Uncle Wayne seems to act "a little strange" that it was because of what he went through during the war. I didn't know what that really meant, except that I was always nagged by regret and embarrassment that my dad was "a little strange." The reason or excuse for his being this way wasn't something that I bothered to spend a lot of time thinking about.

Although emotionally damaged by the war, Wayne lived through it and returned home to become a lifelong insurance agent, not a calling and not a fulfillment of his pre-war plan to go to law school. He needed to put food on the table, so he got a job. He became an insurance agent. He also became a sedentary, depressed, and brooding alcoholic who smoked cheap cigars. That is by no means a balanced or fair portrayal, but these are the things that come to mind first when I think about my father.

My oldest sister, Sarah and I, are separated by thirteen years. Sarah has a completely different and more romanticized image of my father than do I. Sarah saw our father as a strong man, a World War II hero, an avid reader, poetry lover, and an expert horseman. Those aspects of my father had long since faded by the time I came onto the scene, washed away and eroded by the ebb of a beaten down life and the steady flow of alcohol. Early in my life, I do recall hunting and fishing with my father, camping at the cabin at the Farm, and serving as his assistant for mechanical fixes that needed attention around the house. But as I grew into adolescence, those father and son activities faded away. The clearest images that remain in my mind are of my father drinking, brooding, and smoking cigars from morning to sundown in his brown, cracked vinyl living room chair.

Sarah remembers riding horses with my dad out at the Farm. I remember the night I came home from high school basketball practice. Edith for some reason was out of town. I got home and Wayne was waiting for me drunk on the porch. He immediately demanded to know where I'd been. I told him that I had been at basketball practice. He slurred angrily that I was lying! In his drunken state, Wayne took it upon himself to call the coach, the varsity coach, a man who didn't know me. The varsity team did not have practice that night, but I was on the sophomore team. The sophomore team did have practice that night. Why that night my father had all of sudden taken an interest as to my whereabouts, I do not know. He hadn't customarily shown an interest in where I was or what I was doing. He never attended nor was even aware of my school or extracurricular activities. I was infuriated by his drunken inquisition and turned around and left the house. Later that night, when I came home, he was in bed. We never talked further about the matter. He probably didn't remember that it happened.

Sarah remembers ice skating with Dad on the pond at the Farm. I remember being a young boy at a New Year's Eve party at our house. Dad was nearly in a stupor by the time my parents' friends arrived for the party. Wayne was slurring his words, scarcely intelligible. Shortly after folks arrived, he announced that he and my mom were getting divorced. With this announcement, he turned his back on the stunned crowd and stumbled upstairs to bed. Of course they never divorced and, to my knowledge, never even discussed the possibility. But this sort of dark, sloppy, unreasonable behavior is what I came to expect out of my father.

Sarah remembers sailing the family's old-time wooden-, canvas-, and brass-fitted x-boat at Cedar Lake with my father. I remember one grim winter weekend. I was in middle school. My mother implored me to please, *please* call my friend Brian, whose father was a psychiatrist. Wayne was deeply depressed and having an emotional meltdown and needed to talk to Dr. Hintz. I can assure you that that was an uncomfortable call for an insecure fourteen-year-old boy to make. It was during this period when Edith removed the Navy colt .45 from beneath their bed in fear that her husband would use it on himself.

I remember going to great lengths to avoid having my friends over to the house because Dad was probably drunk. I remember the rank smell of his cheap cigars that stayed with me, that clung to my clothes and followed me—embarrassed me—wherever I went. I remember him stumbling from the dock at Cedar Lake, covered in fish guts, blood, and mud. He had fallen and was angry that I had not helped him clean the fish. As he approached, he muttered incoherently and cursed loudly before staggering off to bed despite the fact that the sun was still high in the sky.

These are the things I remember about my father.

However, in fairness to my sister Sarah, her perspective regarding my father is not wrong. But her memories came from a different time and place than were available to me. Also in fairness, others share Sarah's perspective. I have never fully understood it, but my large group of closely knit cousins has, without exception, held my father out as one of their most dear and favorite people. To my cousins, Uncle Wayne was a great storyteller, very kind, caring, loyal, generous, and possessive of the strongest sense of family. In fairness to my own point of view, he wasn't those things to me.

Not long after my mother's death, we moved my father out of his home on 41st Street, the family home of 54 years, in favor of a retirement community. He did not flourish there. He died while my sisters and I were on an excursion in Alaska. Unlike my mother's sudden and unexpected death, my father's life withered away from unknown causes associated with old age and the onset of dementia. I remember one of my sisters once asking my father what he wanted done with his ashes when he died. In response, he slowly wound his index finger in clockwise circles and sputtered that we might as well flush them down the toilet.

And that's kind of how the end of my father's life went for me—no great fanfare, and only faint sorrow in my heart. Truth be told, the source of my sorrow wasn't that he was dead, although I was sad about that. The true source of my sorrow was that he hadn't been a stronger, better father for me. I haven't told anyone that before, but that is the truth. The other truth is that I feel awful for feeling that way.

I don't know what his last moments were like, since I was not there. But I do know that my father died a devout atheist. The most indelible mark that he left on me was his oft-stated belief that "God is for cowards, those too weak to admit that there is no God."

So back to the question: Who am I? Answering that question without talking about what I have done or without reference to other people is difficult. Without using these reference points as a crutch, I must now be totally honest and accountable for the answer.

First, above and beyond all else, I am someone who will do the right thing. I will do what I say I will do. And if I'm not going to do something, I'll say so. Integrity and dependability are, without any doubt, my highest ethical values. I made a decision early on in my professional career that unwavering ethical strength was the most important thing. It's really not hard to do the right thing. It's really not, so long as we simply decide to do only right things.

I also feel strongly that we are connected to each other, those who went before us, those who stand next to us today, and those who will follow. We need to help each other. We need to make a positive difference. I consider myself to be a good and moral person who will always do more than his share.

I have honed a talent and developed the intuitive ability to render quick judgments about people. This is a talent that separates the good bankers from the bad. It's a survival skill. Will this person pay me back? Are they honest? Would they cheat to win? Are they competent? Smart? Are they able to assess situations quickly and make corrective adjustments? Do they know the math of how to make a profit and build a business? How will they respond during tough times, when their back is against the wall? Will they do all that they can to honor their commitments, throw in the towel, or blame someone else?

Being able to assess a person's character and talent, and to do so quickly, is a great skill for a banker to possess. It's not so great when it comes to personal relationships. On a spectrum between directness and kindness, I tend to be very direct, perhaps abrupt, with my judgments. To judge people is an unkind act, but I'm good at it. Good people are good. Bad people are bad. What you've done in the past is who you are. My tendency to judge people creates problems for me when it comes time to forgive. I'm not so good at that. Once I've rendered a judgment about someone, I move on. They should too. There hasn't been much room for others to receive second chances in my world. I know that this is wrong. The inability to forgive has cost me one of the best friendships in my life. I wish I could go back on that one, but I can't. Brice is dead.

The other side of the coin is that I am an introvert living in an extrovert's life. I like solitude and am very comfortable when I am alone. I am terrible at and terribly uninterested by small talk. I prefer to speak only when I have something interesting or important to say. As a boy and young man, people called me shy. This, of course, made me feel inadequate, not up to the task of human interaction. However, throughout the years I have learned to compensate and can render public presentations with apparent ease and zeal. I can engage in conversations and tell stories with the best of them. However, being outspoken is a learned behavior and against my nature. To this day, I remain haunted by an adolescent sense of inadequacy, which others would find hard to believe or see. I am a different person than people think they know.

I am restless. I wish that I were better than I am. Because of my latent sense of inadequacy, I am driven to achieve. Because of that drive, people generally think I am better than I am. At least that's the way I see it. I have considerable doubt and often depressed thoughts. I do not reveal these thoughts to others. I spend equal amounts of time in unhappy and happy states. Again, this would surprise others around me because I do not share these feelings openly. I have a lifelong puzzlement regarding the purpose of life and why I am here. I do not believe in God. My efforts to comprehend the universe and to search for meaning from a rational perspective have borne no fruit.

I am a person who needs to change.

On board. Wheels up.

CHAPTER 3
THE VOYAGE ACROSS

Our tight connection at O'Hare played out just as we'd hoped it would not. A winter storm in Chicago delayed our landing, which in turn caused us to miss our transcontinental connection by the slimmest of margins. We raced frenetically through O'Hare, only to be rewarded with this unwelcome news, news delivered dispassionately by a Queen Latifah doppelganger, our self-proclaimed Angel.

"Plane's gone," she said.

But she went on to declare both her personal and U.S. Air's corporate commitment and competency to assist.

"No worries. I'll take care of y'all."

And she did, in fact, find seats for us on the next

flight to London. Our new flight departed in two hours and was scheduled to arrive in time to make our next connection. Great! Great, except that we lost our roomy, side-by-side aisle seats and were now condemned to eight claustrophobic hours in the dreaded middle seat. I heard my mother's voice: "Well, if that's the worst thing that ever happens to you..." And, as usual, when that saying played in my head, I begin to think about how things could be worse. For instance, what if our bags didn't get re-routed with us? All of our belongings for the next four months were in those bags.

We described our bags and underscored the urgency of the matter. Our Angel nodded. We hung on her every word as she radioed her colleague, Harold, who was unloading luggage from our plane.

"Harold, I'm looking for three bags on Flight 141. I'm looking for three big duffle bags—one green, one brown canvas, and one black. Yeah. Yeah. You got 'em? You got all three of 'em? Well, pull 'em out and send them to British Airlines. Those bags need to go on BA 462. Uh huh. Yeah. You got 'em? Roger that. You da man."

She turned to us and recounted the situation. "Harold's got 'em. You two are all set. Have a great flight."

"Sweet and dandy!" We exchanged high fives with our Angel. With our fire under control, she turned to the next desperate soul in line and went to work delivering their salvation.

Will and I rambled off to our new gate, nourished ourselves with the healthiest fast food available, in time boarded our new flight, and snuggled tightly into our middle seats for all eternity, or at least the next eight hours of it. We took off. Did I mention that I hate middle seats? Irritated and full of angst is not the way I imagined setting sail for my renaissance. I wanted my aisle seat...

But, what's a body to do except make the most of it? And I thought again of my mother: "If that's the worst thing that ever happens to you..." As usual, the thought was not helpful.

I also thought of my mother as I pulled out my kindle from my backpack stuffed beneath my seat. This was a difficult maneuver given my neighbors' gaggle of feet, elbows, knees, and their expanded waistlines. On deck in my kindle was a book entitled *Darling Edith, Dearest Wayne*. My sister Sarah had just transcribed the collection of love letters that Wayne and Edith had written back and forth to each other while separated during World War II. This massive tome, over 700 pages, required a real commitment of time and concentration.

I began, struggling to gain a toehold of interest as I waded through the initial correspondences back and forth between my parents. Wayne and Edith had been married for just nine months when he left for officer training at Tower Hall in Chicago. The officer training was difficult and intellectually challenging. Life alone in Des Moines was uneventful and boring for Edith. They missed each other badly and were both pretty horny. I never heard my mother refer to my father as "Dearest Poosekoop" before, nor my father refer to my mother as "My darling, darling, darling." Some of this stuff was pretty steamy. Should I really be reading it? My sister Julie recounted my mother telling her about these letters with the admonition that they should never, *never* be read.

Oh well, I plodded on, reading the letters somewhat uncomfortably in my voyeuristic roll as our flight sailed across the Atlantic—an hour of reading, a weak movie, the excitement of a bland dinner, an hour of sleep, repeat. So went the flight. Here I was, walled in on both sides by strangers encroaching on my space, stuck in the middle. I closed my eyes and tried to breathe deep, calming breaths. I was in purgatory, in a middle seat, and just beginning a 700 page book, a book which made me uncomfortable to read. The plane slowly made its unending way across the ocean.

I thought to myself that surely the sun would rise tomorrow and when it did I could get off this plane. That's the spirit! Yes, at some point I would be in the future where my middle seat suffering no longer existed. These feeble attempts at positive thinking weren't any more helpful than my mother's "Well if that's the worst thing..." mantra.

Sifting through the random thoughts bouncing around in my head, I grabbed one and held on for a moment. "You know, it wasn't the gremlin's fault. He wasn't the one who uprooted my life," I thought to myself. "It was that old black lady's fault."

I never met her and didn't even know her name. It was over a year ago. Laura and I were eating dinner one night and I asked about her day. She mentioned a patient she worked with that day, a cardiac rehab patient who had very nearly died. The woman, an elderly black woman, nearly saw the white light, but lived for another day. Laura was interviewing this woman to assess her experience and to discuss what changes she might be willing to make to her life. What would she be willing to do in order to stave off another heart trauma? This benign question brought a surprising response.

"You know, I was talking with my daughter. I told her that I almost died today. And I thought to myself, if I knew that this was to be my last day of my life, is this how I would have spent it? I told my daughter absolutely not! Honey, I'm changing everything."

I wondered to myself who this woman was and if she was still alive. I wondered what she was doing today. And I thought how wrong it was that she has no idea the effect she has had on my life. It was that night when I decided that I needed to change everything.

I turned another page in *Darling Edith, Dearest Wayne*.

The flight attendant leaned in. "Chicken or pasta?"

"I'll take the pasta."

CHAPTER 4
THE LANDING

The ensuing events once we touched down at London Heathrow did not cause my optimism to rise.

London was cold and snowy, I suppose typical for the end of January. The snowstorm extended to Amsterdam, and Schiphol's arrivals were suspended. Heathrow is a mess of an airport, with multiple disconnected terminals and an unexpected redundant security checkpoint. We had obviously already passed U.S. security and now stood in a long line waiting to pass a U.K. checkpoint, this one using the metric system. My contact solution did not pass the metric test, too many milliliters, and was confiscated—problem. And things in general were immediately put to the test, things such as the chip in my new credit card and my new smart phone that promised international dialing capabilities.

The first thing I did was dial the rental car agency in Amsterdam to let them know that we were delayed. I guess I passed the international dialing test. At least the phone was ringing. A man answered in a guttural language. I took his tongue to be Dutch and my situation to be pathetic. I told him in English that "I speak only English." I spoke loudly and slowly for affect. He understood my point. We spoke in English, but my comprehension of his English was a pretty iffy thing. Somehow the conversation evolved to agreement that "yes" he understood why I was calling. He was in fact expecting my call.

"Call again when arrive Amsterdam. I drop what do and come get. White van in front Marriott. Very easy find. Just beyond airport."

His message was intended to reassure. But the agreement we forged involved many words, only a few of which were understood by both of us. I was left to wonder, what was it that he'd be doing when I called. Delivering pizza? Repairing a bike? Walking his dog? He didn't seem to be an employee of the car rental agency. In fact, this seemed to be the first time anyone had ever called him regarding a rental car exchange. I had strong doubt that: a) he'd show, or b) we'd find the Marriott. I was much more certain that an unpleasant mess awaited us in Amsterdam, assuming we ever got to Amsterdam, given the weather. As I powered down my phone, I wondered how much that phone call had cost. I had heard the horror stories of people unwittingly running up astronomical roaming charges while traveling abroad.

Dogmatic Slumber

Will and I split a sandwich while we waited in London for the weather to clear. The sandwich was weirdly rare roast beef. We only realized how rare, tartaresque, after the purchase. It was the promise of old English horseradish sauce that sold us on the sandwich, but in the end, all of the ingredients were disappointing. We ate it anyway and did our best to carry on jet-lagged small talk. On the positive side, my new credit card had functioned in the land of British Sterling Pounds.

In due time we were able to board our plane for Amsterdam, a short flight of less than two hours. I harbored concerned about the snow and the time it would take to gather our bags, connect with our driver, work through the details of our car lease, and then drive the 200 km distance from Amsterdam to Groningen. I wasn't looking forward to the prospect of my first driving event in Europe being in the snow at night. I was reminded of my final week at Wells Fargo. Our Credit Officer sent me a lugubrious YouTube compilation of horrible European car accidents, most of them occurring in snow. When I told him that I was leasing a Renault, he told me that was good news. "My wife, Lois, had a Renault. It never started. Maybe you'll be safe after all." Thanks, Lanny.

As it turned out, the snowstorm was only a mild two-inch accumulation. We arrived in Amsterdam with plenty of time to get everything done, including completing the drive to Groningen before dark. Or so I thought. We were met by a slightly ominous revelation as we cleared EU customs. My scheduled 105 day stay in the EU exceeded the 90 day allowance. The stern customs agent informed me of the impending violation. No problem today, but one that would be waiting for me when it came time to return to the states in May. "We'll cross that bridge when we come to it," I decided, lacking any better forethought in the moment. Getting a visa at this point would be time-consuming, expensive, and perhaps impossible.

Undeterred, Will and I cleared customs and proceeded to the baggage claim carousel to collect our bags. We waited. We waited. And we waited. We waited until the last lonely bag was claimed and the carousel made a few empty cycles. It slowed to a stop. Our bags were lost. As it turned out, our Angel in Chicago was a blowhard incompetent, either that or a cruel, dark-hearted servant of Satan. Despite her assurances to the contrary, our bags never made it to our plane. They were lost somewhere in an unmapped stretch of limbo between US Airways and British Airways.

We made our way to the lost bag claims department, where we waited our turn to visit with the tall, standoffish, blonde baggage claim representative. First and foremost, she made it clear that she had no emotional attachment to our problem. This was my first encounter with the Dutch. It turns out that almost all Dutch people are tall, blonde, beautiful, and indifferent. To the Dutch, all problems are avoidable, including yours, if only you'd planned more thoughtfully. Here we stood at this young woman's indifferent mercy.

"Did you purchase travel insurance?"

"No."

"That was an unfortunate choice, wasn't it? Insurance would cover your loss. I hope that we can find your bags. Where are you staying?"

"We're driving to Groningen and staying at a hotel there."

"Where?"

"Groningen."

"I don't understand."

"Groningen."

"What."

"Our bags are lost! We're not staying in Amsterdam. We're driving to Groningen. Groningen. We are driving to Groningen. GRONINGEN."

I simply could not say the name of this town in such a way that she could comprehend, this despite the fact that Groningen is a pretty substantial-sized city, maybe 180,000 people, just a two-hour drive north from where we stood. As instructed, I produced our baggage claim documentation, drew crude renderings of our bag, and wrote the name and address of our hotel on our claim form.

She casually looked at the form. "Oh. Groningen." she said, forming a strange raspy noise from deep in her throat. Her pronunciation sounded more like a hack than a word.

"Exactly! Groningen!" I said trying to mimic her hack.

She assured us that the bags, if found, would be delivered to our hotel. However, her assurance was vague and cloaked in broken English. I was left with strong doubt that we would ever see our bags again. Will's six-month, two-duffle-bag luggage collection of belongings and my four-month, one-duffle-bag assortment of clothes might never be found. I tried one last time to underscore the gravity of our situation. She shrugged indifference and we schlepped off, demoralized.

Our fortunes soon took a positive turn. Happily, the Airport Marriott was in fact an easy find. The young, bespectacled driver and his white van were in fact there to meet us. English was hard to come by as we climbed into the van and attempted small talk. We drove for quite a while, ending up at a parking lot in a remote and dark industrial district, seemingly in the middle of nowhere and everywhere at the same time. Once we arrived, we reviewed the lengthy stack of papers constituting the lease contract. We received cursory instructions on how to operate the car, and the young man waved as we drove off into the dusk in our brand new black Renault. Fortified that we were on the ground in Europe, we set our sights north to Groningen.

We travelled light, unfettered by baggage. The roads were slushy and threatened to turn to ice as the short winter day darkened. Two hours later, we reached Groningen, where it was dark and snowing. An incredible spectacle embraced us as we entered the city's ring of medieval canals. There were hundreds of people on bicycles making their way through the dark, snowy streets. I've never seen anything like it: no cars, only bikes. Everyone, EVERYONE in Groningen bicycles to wherever and everywhere they are going. The streets of Groningen brim with throngs of bell-ringing Dutch bikers regardless of how horrible the weather, or how dark the night. *Ding! Ding! Ping! Ping!* There is no doubt that bikers own the road. Pedestrians and motorists beware.

We followed the car's GPS guide to our hotel, winding our way alongside Groningen's half-frozen canals, all the time ducking and dodging the herds of hearty bicyclists. Our hotel was situated near the Grote Market, a historic market square with pubs, shops, restaurants, and a spectacular high-rising bell tower. Under normal circumstances, this would have been a terrific place to walk about. But without coats and just the shirts on our backs to keep us warm, we ventured out only a few short blocks at a time, and then only for necessities such as contact solution and food. Without hats and coats, walking to even a nearby destination on Groningen's winter streets was horrible. The return trip, with defenses worn down, was life-threatening.

Things were expensive here. For example, parking: Street parking was a limited commodity and extremely expensive. Parking meters required hourly feeding 24 hours a day. Our only option was to rent a compact parking stall beneath the hotel for 25€ per night. By compact, I mean really tight, no more than four inches of clearance on either side. It took five minutes of turning back and forth for me to successfully maneuver the car into the stall. I soon learned that bicycles were welcomed in Groningen, automobiles were not. Motorists were in fact punished by a complex ringed network of streets that were two-way for bicycles but one-way or often impassable by car. Parking, forget about it!

With driving scorned and walking without hats and coats painful, Will and I shuffled only modestly around Groningen. Our sojourns from the hotel were short and few. We did take a day trip to the old, fortified city of Bourtange near the German border, which was both cool and cold. We saw windmills in the countryside and boats on the canals. We ate at a few nice pubs and restaurants and streamed an Iowa Hawkeye basketball loss. We passed the time.

But truth be told, Groningen was a dark and gloomy place. At least this was the case this time of year in our laundry-less, jet-lagged state. Expenses were adding up. Parking was 75€ for our three nights. We were in a touristy but seasonally vacant section of town where meals cost maybe 20€ each. The hotel wasn't cheap either. In my mind I tossed about the concern that our bags might be permanently lost. Neither US Air nor British Airways knew where our bags were, and they pointed fingers at each other as to who was responsible for losing them. Even if our bags were miraculously found, how would they find their way to where we were, several hours north of Amsterdam in Groningen, a village our baggage claim lady had a difficult time getting her mind around? How much would it cost to replace all of this stuff, including Will's lifetime collection of soccer gear? Could we replace it? How would we? I imagined a gruesome shopping excursion to buy everything that we'd need for the next several months. Maybe I'd get lucky and someone would sneak up from behind and hit me with a blunt object first, putting me out of my misery.

I've been without a paycheck for less than two weeks. Here I was paying 25 Euros a night for parking and faced with the possible need to shop for thousands of dollars of lost clothing. I had plenty of money, but the sensation of reversed cash flow was foreign to me. This was my mindset as I donned the same shirt and underwear for the fourth day.

And on the fourth day there was light! Pure, unadulterated joy was delivered to us in the form of three well-worn but familiar duffle bags. Glory! I have never been so glad as to see those bags sitting behind the reception desk in the lobby. All was good with the world and our spirits were lifted. We took our bags up to the room and dug for fresh underwear and socks.

Once we received our bags, the mostly grim and desperate feelings we had been carrying turned much more positive. But an undeniable sense of foreboding was also building with each passing day, culminating with tomorrow. Tomorrow I was leaving Groningen. My son would be on his own and I would begin my solitary journey to the Abbey in Pontlevoy. From afar I had looked forward to this day. However, now, as tomorrow approached, I had an enormous sense of gravity. Something irreversible was about to occur. This was it. Separate ways, my son.

And so, early in the grayness of the next morning, Will and I went down to the car together. In a few hours he was meeting up with the other exchange students for the first time. I was shoving off for an eight-hour drive through Holland, Belgium, and France to the small village of Pontlevoy. As we said goodbye, I was overcome with an unmanageable surge of emotion that I have only experienced a few times before in my life. The first time was when Laura and I dropped Audrey off at Beloit College in Wisconsin. The next time was when we held Sophie, our chocolate lab, as she was put to sleep. There was the time we dropped Will off at college. And now this farewell.

In each instance it was a matter of saying goodbye coupled with a heavy sensation that something that I loved was changing irreversibly. As I hugged Will goodbye, I had to compose myself to speak. This was difficult. Things were changing, forever. Rather than a sense of new beginning, I felt an almost unbearable sense of loss. Things were changing and it was so uncertain what the new world would look like. Letting go of your children, letting them test their wings and fly, is one of life's most difficult things. The difficulty of that act on that cold gray morning in Groningen was compounded by the fact that I myself was jumping off a cliff at the same time and embarking in a new direction.

As much as I had hoped to be prepared for the emotion of this moment, I was not. I held back tears as long as I could, but lost that battle. With a soft goodbye, I engaged the Renault, worked back and forth out of the tight parking space, and waved at Will. He and I made unforgettable eye contact through sorrowful tears, but tears also filled with love. I pulled out of the garage onto the snowy streets of Groningen and accelerated slowly, heading away towards something, something that I did not know. I glanced back and forth in the rearview mirror at Will as I pulled away. I worried if he would be all right, or not. But the time had come. He was on his own. And so was I.

Will Mackaman on Gronigen canal

Chapter 5
Arrival

I had romanticized a solitary drive across Netherlands and Belgium, a casual and charming route through the European countryside. Instead the trip was all business, mostly an unrewarding 130km per hour drudge along the busy four-lane Auto Route. As I drove, I was ensconced in the darkness of low-hanging clouds and pounded by heavy rain. The dissonance between the imagined and the actual Belgium in particular was striking. I had envisioned Belgium to imbue a blend of French and Flemish country appeal. However, the part of Belgium that was visible to me from the Auto Route was mostly a wet, gray, industrial yuck.

I became concerned as I crossed the border from Belgium to France. My female GPS guide seemed intent on taking me not around but rather directly into the belly of the beast, Paris. Traffic thickened during my hour-long approach. I listened intently to every command as she directed me towards the congested roadways, busy intersections, incomprehensible roundabouts, and abrupt exit ramps of Paris. I had no idea how to wend my way through Paris without her guidance, so I clutched the wheel tightly and eked my way through the city's complex and foreboding traffic flow.

Driving in France is fast and furious. In Paris the roads are small and tight, many built without foresight that someday the automobile would be invented. Streets are not organized in north/south grids. Rather, they bend and turn wherever they choose. Street names are long, multisyllabic, and impossible to remember. The cars are small, with nervous, high RPM motors. The French love to ride your bumper. The guy behind you isn't comfortable until you're uncomfortable. *En guard!*

In France, traffic signs are alarming and incomprehensible. The upside down triangle with arrows going both ways with an exclamation point means that you need to stop to let oncoming traffic pass (Now, before you die!). I never did figure out what the circled skull with a line through it meant, but it disturbed me greatly. Intermittent horn beeps and longer, angrier horn blasts blare from all directions. The intersections are free-for-alls. The roundabout at the Arch de Triumph has fourteen bustling streets spoking into a circular traffic flow, the center of which has eight hectic and unmarked lanes. Pity the poor soul that gets pushed into the innermost circle. Like Dante's inferno, there's no escape from that labyrinth.

Indeed, Paris is a very foreign and precarious place to drive. I remained on extreme alert and followed my guide's directions blindly and exactly. A breakdown, an accident, lost asking for directions—I played out all of these scenarios in my head. They all ended badly.

Thankfully, over time the traffic began to thin as I emerged from the bowels of Paris intact and heading south. I'd been on the road for six hours by now with two hours strong yet to go. South of Paris, I began to encounter a series of unpleasant obstacles, the unmanned French toll ways—exact change or credit cards only! The instructions for rendering cash payment were complex and obscured by the French language. My credit card worked unpredictably and only at every other toll booth. When it didn't work, I was forced to push the intercom button for help. Then I had to explain my predicament, in my best French, to an unseen attendant as the line of angry French drivers grew behind me.

"Mon carte de credit ne marche pas."

"Pardon?"

"MON CARTE DE CREDIT NE MARCHE PAS!!!"

Sooner or later these desperate and escalating conversations forced a head-shaking attendant to venture across the traffic to see what in the world my problem was. Somehow, by hook or by crook, by cash or by credit, I was allowed to pass. I didn't keep track, but I think it took a lot of money.

The winter day was short, and the farther I drove, daylight began to fade into darkness. An hour or so south of Paris, I gratefully departed the French Auto Route and escaped her intolerant toll booths. I began following and crisscrossing the Cher River, traveling more slowly along progressively smaller roadways. By the time I climbed the hill to Pontlevoy, it was dark.

Pontlevoy was a very small village situated on the plateau both above and between the Loire and the Cher Rivers. My cousin Doug had put me in touch with a local connection of his, named Alban. Alban, via email, had helped me to secure a rental home in Pontlevoy. Alban assured me that this was a very nice house, owned by a good friend of his. The house was very clean and a great bargain at just 550€ per month, including heat. Electricity is expensive in France, so having heat included in the rent was significant.

Upon arriving in Pontlevoy, I had instructions to call my landlord, Monsieur Marc Barret, so that he could meet me at the house and give me the key. However, the house and street number didn't register with my GPS guide. And when I dialed Monsieur Barret's phone number, my cell phone produced a "no service" message. Hmmm. Now what? I pulled up and parked next to a small, darkly lit brasserie. The exterior sign read "Le Commerce." It was Sunday night and there were no signs of life in the village. The brasserie, while dark, was the only sign of a commercial business that I could see.

I turned off the car, took a fortifying deep breath, and shifted into French parley mode. I had taken French classes in high school, traveled to France a handful of times, and brushed up with Pimsleur before this trip. Nonetheless this was my first crack at the French language in quite a while. I was about to dive in headfirst. I equate my French vocabulary to that of a seven-year-old. My transition to past or future tense is tenuous at best. By necessity I awkwardly work to couch everything in the present tense, the here and now.

As I opened the door to the brasserie, I could see that the lights had been turned down for a reason. It was not open for business. However, there were three individuals quietly saddled up to the bar along with the proprietor, all smoking. I could tell that they did not expect or necessarily welcome a stranger at this hour.

I grabbed my courage and spoke, "Bon soire, tout le monde."

"Bon soire," replied the proprietor with a questioning look. He was a young man. I made note of his tallish, slender build, short, wavy black hair, dark brown eyes, and slight, upturned smile at both corners of his mouth.

I spoke to him. "Est-ce que vous connesez mon cousin, Doug Mackaman?" This was my best effort at, "Are you familiar with my cousin, Doug Mackaman?" I hoped that most of the people in the village would know Doug based upon his role at the Abbey. I further hoped that my family connection might bring about a willingness to assist.

"Pardon?"

I repeated myself. We continued our nascent conversation, both of us searching for comprehension. "Est-ce que vous connesez mon cousin, Doug Mackaman?"

"Oh, oui," the man replied.

"Je m'appelle David, David Mackaman."

"Enchanté. Je m'appelle Julien."

"Enchanté. Julien, est-ce que vous parlez Anglais?"

"Yes, I do."

"Bon. C'est mieux pour moi."

We shook hands and I explained that I was trying to call my landlord, Monsieur Barret, but that my cell phone was not working.

"Do you know him?" I asked.

Julien did not, but he offered to dial the number and was able to connect. As I tried to follow the rapid, incomprehensible French exchange that was happening over the phone, I knew that I was in way over my head. Julien hung up and told me that Monsieur Barett would be here in ten minutes. He lived out in the country. From behind the bar Julien poured me a complimentary beer and we exchanged pleasantries while we waited for Monsieur Barett to arrive. We spoke mostly in English. I tried to inject French where I could. And so it was that early on, at this little brasserie named Le

Commerce, I had found my first friend in Pontlevoy: Julien. Over the coming weeks and months, Julien and I would come to know each other well as friends.

As promised, Monsieur Barret, Marc, strode through the door and into the small, dimly lit room. He was tall, smiling, and wore a brown leather-brimmed hat over his thinning brown hair. I immediately realized that Alban had misled me. Alban had assured me that Marc's English was quite good. I now knew that Marc spoke no words in English and only two letters: O and K. However, despite our language barriers, I would later learn that I had just met another person who would, over time, become a good friend.

"Vous me suivez a la maison, OK?" Marc asked. (Follow me to the house.)

"D'accord," I responded.

I followed him, he in his car and me in mine, just a short block down the narrow, slightly sloping, medieval street leading from Le Commerce to the house. Marc stopped and we parked in the misty darkness. We stood outside of an immense and seemingly ancient wooden gate, maybe ten feet high, which guarded the courtyard. In the dark of night I could see that the house was tall, three stories. It was the last house on the street, but connected by adjacent walls to a small line of homes that stretched up the street towards Le Commerce. The connected buildings were indistinguishable in color, all off-white or faded natural stucco. The wooden gate to the courtyard was directly across the street from a huge iron gate leading to the Abbey grounds.

Marc concentrated and muttered in French as he wrestled with the locked gate, turning the key once and then again with difficulty. I gathered from our conversation that this gate was to remain closed and locked at all times. Why? I couldn't imagine. The village certainly seemed peaceful enough. However, I would later learn that transient gypsies, the Romas, lived in the area and were known to steal cars and whatever else they could as they moved around the region, rooted from one squatter's campground to the next. The perceived gypsy risk, coupled with centuries of relentless foreign army invasions, had caused most of the villagers to protect their homes by gating the entrance to their courtyards.

Marc finally wrestled the lock open. He locked it and demonstrated the mechanics again. Now it was my turn. With his coaching, I tried to unlock the gate on my own. It was cold and dark. And the battle with the ancient, finicky lock was a struggle. But I ultimately emerged victorious. Victory came with patience and with a jiggling of the key just so, a creaky turn once, a regroup, and then a second jiggling of the key, a second turn just so, and voila! You're a winner!

After mastering the courtyard gate, I walked with Marc into the darkness of the courtyard. We trudged across the wet, crunching gravel towards the back door of the house. The lock to the back door of the house required the same level of attention and particularity as the front gate. So again we worked together, him teaching and me learning this challenge. Finally, with the lock lessons behind us, we entered the house.

Just like outside, it was cold inside the house as well. We walked up a creaking wooden staircase with two landings, holding onto a well-worn pale green handrail as we made our way. As we progressed, we occasionally came to, and turned on, a couple of Edison-vintage lights to guide our way.

The house was a primitively restored 300-year-old building once operated as a grain merchant business. It was divided into three stories. The stairway between the floors was unheated and closed off to each floor in order to provide the best possible chance of retaining heat in the living areas. The ground floor was comprised of a simple entryway, a single closet, and a primal unheated bathroom. The second floor had a kitchen, a connected dining room, an austere open sitting area, and a spare bedroom with two twin beds and a fireplace which "ne marche pas"—didn't work. The third floor was a mostly vacant, sparsely furnished open space with a low, slope-roofed double bedroom and a second bathroom, this one heated with a shower stall. The entry to the upstairs bedroom was low, so low that I had to duck beneath the crossbeam to avoid bumping my forehead.

The home's walls were made of thick, exposed white bricks smeared with an unusual orange-tinged stain. The ceiling was white, with exposed, rough wooden crossbeams. Uneven, sometimes cracked red tiles covered the floor. Furnishings were antique and rough. The kitchen met Webster's definition of basic but included a clothes washer, no dryer. The sources of warmth for the entire house were a few strategically placed electric wall heaters. They labored with difficulty to keep up with the cold radiating through the stone walls and leaking in through the windows.

After our brief and verbally challenging tour of the home, Marc and I sat down at the kitchen table. He pointed to the wall in the sitting room opposite the kitchen table. I understood him to say that if I stood close to that wall I could perhaps pirate a weak internet connection ("Le Weefee") from my neighbor. I later learned this to be the case. Under just the right conditions, occasionally depending upon wind, weather, and maybe sunspot activity, I could, in fact, gather a weak, erratic internet connection through the thick walls that I shared with my neighbor.

Seated together at the table, Marc and I went through the remainder of our business dealings. I signed a lease agreement and paid 1,650€ cash rent for the next three months. I only comprehended about half of what Marc was telling me, and he even less of what I was trying to say to him, but we were both actually enjoying the effort to communicate. I was able to explain to him that I needed a few groceries yet that night. The small market in Pontlevoy was closed. Where could I go?

Marc told me that there was a small market in the neighboring village of Montrichard where I could get what I needed. Our business done, Marc and I got into our cars and I followed him in the direction of Montrichard, a seven km downhill drive towards the Cher River. At night it was a perilous road, dark and narrow. Marc guided me in the direction of Montrichard before he turned off on the country lane leading to his house. I waved au revoir and found my way to the market at Montrichard, where I bought cereal, coffee, a six-pack of Belgian beer, potato chips, bread, and cheese. With those items of sustenance in hand, I headed back up the hill through the dark to Pontlevoy.

I returned to my new home and, with patience and my best Zen-like karma, approached the locked gate. With an "it will work" attitude and considerable effort, I was able to unlock both the courtyard gate and back door to the house. I walked into the house and up the creaky stairs leading to the vacant kitchen and sitting room. The house was empty. The hollow echo of my footsteps on the tiles reverberated off the thick stone walls. The walls were cold to the touch. The sparseness was undeniable. Outside it was cold and dark. It wasn't as dark inside, but it was still cold. I had to stand very near the heaters to feel their warmth.

I tried my cell phone again to maybe call Laura or to check in with Will, only to once again receive a "no service" message. My medieval internet connection was not cooperating either. I had no music, no TV. Cousin Doug and the students were not arriving for a few more days. I knew no one within a roughly 4,000 mile radius of this spot. I was as alone as I've ever been. I opened and poured a lonely bottle of beer.

What have I done?

I resisted the impulse to dwell on that question, but at the same time could not put it out of my mind. I sat down, fired up my kindle, and began reading more from *Darling Edith, Dearest Wayne*. Then I went to bed.

Chapter 6
Pontlevoy: The Early Days

I got out of bed my first morning in Pontlevoy and awoke alone to a cold, clean slate. I looked out my front window. From there I could see the parish church directly across the street. The church's bells had announced the beginning of the new day just a short time ago with seven resounding chimes. An hour later there would be eight, and so on until 7:00 that evening. The church bells rang nearby, from just across the street. And yet, they seemed to toll from a faraway land and time. I looked past the parish church. Just behind it I could see the Abbey, a massive, medieval structure with a towering church steeple flanked by flying buttresses. An imposing black iron fence surrounded what I could see of the Abbey's extensive grounds.

Turning towards the two windows along the back wall of the house, I looked out upon my gated courtyard. My black Renault was parked there. The courtyard was peaceful, if not a meticulously tended clos. It might have been more beautiful during a different season. During the winter, the gravel was frozen together and covered by a visible layer of frost. The anonymous plants were leafless and hibernating; the rough patches of grass, dormant.

I brewed a pot of coffee, poured a bowl of cereal, took a shower, and rattled around the house for a bit before setting out to explore. As I left my house, I tried the Abbey's south gate. It was locked. Up the street, the brasserie where I had stopped last night, Le Commerce, was also closed. I walked another block to the boulangerie and went inside. The bakery was quaint, warm, and teeming with sweet, buttery smells. Sugary and yeasty pleasures crowded the glass counter. The young woman behind the counter smiled sweetly as I ordered two flakey croissants and a fresh baguette.

I left the boulangerie and continued a few blocks farther to the Cocci Marché, where I bought a couple of apples, a pound of butter, a small wheel of brie, and a bottle of red wine for dinner that evening. The owner voiced concern about my choice of butter. "Avec sel?!" Yes, with salt. No need for alarm.

On the way home I encountered a scant few villagers and offered a few bonjours. By and large, it was a cold and lonely walk. I passed Pontlevoy's World War I monument, which was inscribed with the names of village lives lost in the war. It was a long list of names.

I also noticed several large placards, black and white photographs, hung on exterior building walls throughout the village. These photographs were presented in the form of an outside museum, the Musée dans la Rue. The Musée was a veritable time machine, a nostalgic assembly of photographs taken many years ago by a local watchmaker named Louis Clergeau—a fat-tired bicycle race from Pontlevoy to Chaumont, a parade of citizens through once vibrant streets, people standing in front of store façades long ago shuttered, musical performances by young students studying then at the Abbey, now old men and women or, more likely, deceased. Wistful, almost ghostly, the photographs harkened back to long gone days when a provincial village of 1,500 could function as a self-sustaining community. Times had changed. While Pontlevoy was a charming village, it was easy to see that it was struggling to thrive in the modern era. Commerce was sputtering. Many businesses had closed. Several buildings were shuttered here and there. I presumed that many of the village's young had departed to live in larger cities with more cosmopolitan offerings.

Making my way back in the direction of my house, I approached the Abbey's north gate, ajar but no signs of life. I entered the gate and walked around the grounds past an enormous tree. The tree's drooping canopy served as a giant umbrella for a large section of the courtyard. The tree, a Cedar of Lebanon, was planted during 1776 in honor of Louis XVI's ascension to the throne. Overall, the Abbey's grounds were extensive and included an adequately, if not finely manicured, bousquet garden of conical-shaped evergreens.

I walked through the courtyard, past the cedar tree, towards the Abbey's high, heaven-reaching chapel. I entered. My lonely footsteps echoed from floor to ceiling as I walked. A musty odor permeated the dank stone walls. I could sense and smell the centuries of worship, remnants of lit candles and burnt incense, sickly sweet. Along the back wall of the apse was a row of ancient organ pipes that had played their last notes many years ago. Behind the altar was a statue of a white virgin holding her child. The statue paid homage to the story of a knight, Gelduin de Chaumont. Gelduin founded the Abbey upon his return from the Crusades. Legend has it that Gelduin's ship was caught in a horrendous storm. He prayed for salvation, and those prayers were answered by the white virgin. In exchange for saving his life, Gelduin promised the virgin that he would build a church in Pontlevoy upon his return. He kept his promise.

Exiting the chapel, I went back into the courtyard and approached the Abbey's other dominant structure, its monastery, a double-winged, two-story row of windowed rooms that look out upon the Abbey grounds. The main door at the end of the first wing was unlocked. There were still no signs of anyone, so I quietly and discretely entered. My footsteps reverberated as I walked through the monastery's meagerly furnished, cavernous hallways. I could sense the ghostly presence of past souls whose footsteps had preceded mine centuries ago. As I walked I took an inventory of what I could see and what I already knew about this place.

Monks lived in the monastery for many centuries, centuries ago. Today this was where the students resided, attended class, and studied during their time at the Abbey. Over time the Abbey evolved into and from many things: a monastery, a military academy, a leper sanctuary, an acclaimed international school (George Washington's grandson matriculated here), and an ignoble abandoned building. That was the state of affairs when Doug stumbled upon the Abbey some twenty years ago. The utilities had been shut off, windows were broken, varmints had moved into residence, and the grounds were overgrown and unattended. Doug, dreaming big, brought together an American university, an investor from the States, a French bank, and the French government to buy and fund the Abbey's restoration back to life.

Once purchased and at least adequately restored, Doug hit the recruiting trail with fervor. He was energetic, persistent, and successful in opening up an ongoing flow of students and professors to come the Abbey to teach and learn. And come they did, in droves, beginning in 2001. I tried to imagine that first night of classes when the Abbey lights were ceremoniously relit. The village's aging heart surely gained an extra beat that night. The Abbey has always been the village's heart and soul, the core of its provincial allure.

The Abbey and its environs are authentically ancient and rich with history. I could still see the marks where flames kissed the Abbey's back wall during World War II. Doug shares the sweet story once told to him by an elderly woman in the village. She was a young girl the night the Germans marched in to occupy the town. She joined hand in hand with the other villagers as they stood in a circle. They sobbed and watched as the Germans' ignited flames bent on destroying the Abbey, and on breaking the village's spirit. But as the flames approached, just as they met the Abbey's walls, the fire fell back and died. The villagers rejoiced. The Abbey was spared.

True, the Abbey was spared from the fire, but it remains today in the financial frying pan. The program that Doug orchestrates is really just a tenant of the building for a few months out of the year. The physical facility is owned by a private investor from Michigan. During the remainder of the year, when the Abbey Program is not in session, the facility is irregularly occupied and generally underutilized. The mortgage taken out to buy and restore the property is substantial, the cash flow meager. Building maintenance has been abundantly deferred. Several outbuildings have been left exposed to the elements. Interior plaster and paint are chipped in many places. Some of the windows are cracked; most need painting and caulking. The thick stone walls and floors radiate a chilling embrace. Leaky doors and windows create a discernible wind chill. Attempts to retrofit modern conveniences have been met with limited success. The huge kitchen where the students cook is industrial and accommodating. The laundry room is functional, if not modern. The wireless internet connection is met with strong resistance by the Abbey's three-foot stone walls. Spotty reception and system crashes are continual student banes.

The Abbey is, quite simply, a diamond in the rough, its ills nothing that several million dollars more couldn't fix. There will never be enough money, and everyone understands that. People love her just the way she is, a well-worn guardian of nearly 1000 years of history.

I completed my tour. Having seen most of the village highlights, I continued walking back towards my house, feeling very alone. I wish then that I could have seen the future. Soon the students and staff would arrive and begin to form a close, caring community; Julien from Le Commerce would become such a good friend; the ladies at the boulangerie would come to recognize and welcome me; Francois at the Cocci Marché would greet me enthusiastically, "David!"; and villagers on the street would smile warmly and often stop to chat. But these relationships did not yet exist. I had no idea of how warmly Pontlevoy would come to welcome me.

In need of companionship, I sent a message to Keenon, the Abbey's student advisor. Keenon was a twenty-something-year-old black man from Mississippi. Though our paths hadn't crossed during my tour of the Abbey, I knew that Keenon had been at the Abbey for a few days getting things set for the students. I asked him if he wanted to join me for dinner. We agreed to meet at Le Commerce that evening. Marianne, the woman who managed the Abbey's physical facility, would join us.

Keenon was the only black man in Pontlevoy, so he was easy enough to spot when he and Marianne walked into the restaurant to join me for dinner. He was large-boned, with a shaved head and a smiling personality, a young and jubilant soul. Keenon had studied abroad last year and fallen in love with exploring foreign cultures, particularly England. He brought an energetic grasp of social media to the table, along with an enthusiastic international awareness.

Marianne was a French native who spoke brilliant English. She had a quirky, but adorable, little bug-eating French bulldog, Hypnos, who followed her everywhere. Marianne was a mysterious soul with a complicated life story that spanned many continents. I couldn't follow all of her story, but I gathered that she'd rather be somewhere else other than Pontlevoy. Marianne could have been cast as a terrific black-dressed femme fatale. She was glamorous and held her emotions very close. The emotions she did reveal were difficult to read. She shifted back and forth—depending upon the moment—between sending friendly and passively unwelcoming vibes. I liked her.

In any event, the three of us laughed and got to know each other over dinner that evening. Keenon in particular would become a close friend.

After dinner I went back to my house and pulled *Darling Edith, Dearest Wayne* back off the shelf, reading several passages before going to sleep. I was definitely getting pulled into the book. In a very real way, I felt as though I were meeting my parents for the very first time. Their story was captivating, which was not a term I had ever used to describe my parents.

I woke up my second morning in Pontlevoy and leapt into motion by initiating my plan to exercise regularly. I charted a circular running route through the village and out to fringes of the countryside. I ran this route a couple of times each week. The first couple of passes on the route were cold, huffy, and puffy.

However, over time I began to notice my endurance extending.

In concert with my exercise routine, I set out to eat fewer, healthier meals, just two per day. I would eat breakfast every day (with fruit) and later eat either lunch or dinner. Those main meals included small amounts of starch, lesser portions of protein, and a winter vegetable or salad. This routine might mean a large chef salad at Le Commerce for lunch or a simple sautéed chicken breast prepared at home with Basque or Provençal sauce, pasta, and salad.

The idea was basic, to eat generally nutritious foods in small portions and to exercise daily. This was a significant intended aspect of my journey, to consciously take actions to improve my health and vitality. During my youth I had been able to be active and healthy without truly working at it. I had been a runner most of my life, albeit a slowing one with now-tender knees. I ran the Twin Cities Marathon ten years ago. I biked 30-40 miles, sometimes 50-60 miles, at a time fairly regularly during seasons that would permit. I played tennis weekly. I walked our Labrador, Maya, three miles or more daily with Laura.

But I knew that I was at least ten pounds overweight, slowing down, and suspected that measurements such as weight, blood pressure, and cholesterol levels would begin to trend in the wrong direction absent a commitment. So I went to work on the physical aspects of my being during my early days at Pontlevoy.

The Abbey's flying buttresses

The Abbey monastery

Dogmatic Slumber

Pontlevoy: Le Commerce, looking towards chez moi just down the street.

Courtyard view of my house and the Parish Church

Chapter 7
The People

On the third day, others began to arrive, which brought a welcome change. The first two days were pretty much on my own. At times I felt as though I was stranded on an island, a beautiful but solitary place, surrounded by an empty ocean, and all alone. However, as the students and faculty began to arrive, a cast of lively characters began to swim ashore. The first to arrive was Doug. Doug's itinerary for the term was to spend two weeks kicking things off, fly back to the states, and then return for the program's final two-week wrap-up. Keenon and I were together in the Abbey office when Doug stormed into the room.

"Salut!" Comment ça va?!" he bellowed. I rose to hug him.

Doug is of medium height and build; his smile is XXXL. He has medium-cut brown hair and wears glasses with thick black frames, essentially Wayfarers without tint. He dresses casually but with a noticeable euro-style, vintage leather boots with zippers, jeans with the bottoms rolled up above his ankles, a brown leather jacket, and a Burberry plaid scarf. Doug has been known to carry a man-bag without regret.

The embodiment of exuberance, Doug is both blood and a great friend. He is also a true testament to positivity. Through the sheer power of his own spirit, Doug always seems to cause things to break his way. The Abbey is a great example of that. We have a family saying that Doug always manages to land with his bum in the butter. Doug is bombastic, brilliant, and fun. Excitement! Energy! Passion! Hilarity! These attributes cling to Doug tenaciously and follow him wherever he goes.

Doug founded the Abbey Program as well as two other foreign study programs, all born through the parenting of his ingenuity and charisma. To endlessly recruit students and faculty, semester after semester, must require energy and a tireless work ethic. But Doug makes it look effortless, and he has developed the rare talent of getting other people excited about sweating the details, not his strength. In that sense I see him as a modern day Tom Sawyer.

Doug took me around and introduced me to the teaching staff. I was impressed. Over time I would come to know each of the professors well and personally. This was a new realm for me, to live among academicians. These individuals were warm, interested, and interesting. The conversations with this group were much different than the business dialogues to which I was accustomed. Conversations about Molière, Balzac, or Zola over coffee, about the Renaissance, Irish playwrights, or French cinema over a glass of wine were stimulating and much different than to-the-point lunch meetings or phone calls with business owners to talk about interest rates, employment statistics, or business trends.

Kevin, the English teacher, was maybe 30 years old, give or take. He had collar-length, wavy black hair pulled casually behind his ears. Kevin's build was slight. Girls would describe his appearance and calm voice as "dreamy." Kevin wore only neutral colors and usually had on his well-worn brown suede sport coat. He was soft spoken, articulate, and well-read. Kevin was an author. He penned one novel, winner of an Australian book award, and occasionally wrote features for an Australian newspaper. He was also well-versed in film, particularly foreign film.

Kevin and his wife, Jennifer, who would join us later in the semester, both grew up in Louisiana. Through what I took as conscious effort, both Kevin and Jennifer had left behind any noticeable trace of a southern accent. They travelled together as citizens of the world, not as people raised in America's south. They resided in Australia, but lived in Paris for the six months leading up to the Abbey term. Kevin was awarded a six-month scholarship by the Australian government that allowed Jennifer and him to live in Paris while he worked on writing his second novel.

Jennifer was thin and beautiful with long brown hair. She would probably be thin no matter what, but the driving reasons for her thin build were her multiple food allergies. These allergies caused her to subsist on a very limited and, unfortunately, tasteless diet. Despite that, Jennifer was very cheery and, like Kevin, articulate. She was sweet, demure, normally smiling, and could match Kevin's intellectualism pound for pound and, in fact, up the ante. She was working on her PhD from a university in Australia and was at a stage where she was finishing her thesis and the required authorship of her first novel. Together, Kevin and Jennifer were two of my best friends during my time in Pontlevoy.

Ben taught Islamic History. He was a single, middle-aged man on staff at the University of Southern Mississippi. He had a short, grizzled beard and matted grey hair flattened beneath one of two hats, either a Boston Red Sox baseball cap or a black felt English driving cap. During most of the term, Ben owned a deep, lingering cold. The affliction kept him constantly teetering back and forth between his deathbed and Pontlevoy's cold winter streets. It was a common sight to see Ben moving slowly between his house and the Abbey in hunched, wracking shuffles. Ben was the expert of experts on Islam, particularly North African Muslim culture and history. Tunis was his Mecca. Ben was a human Google search on North Africa and the particular details of Muslim history and culture. He knew everything about this subject and loved to talk about it. For me, a little bit of Muslim history went a long way, but I certainly respected Ben's grasp of the subject.

Catherine was our French History professor for the first half of the term. She was a diminutive young woman, maybe 26-27 years old, and very slight with long sand-colored hair and thin wire-rimmed glasses. By slight, I'd guess that she was maybe five feet tall and weighed less than 100 pounds. Catherine was a very intense person, at all times the brightest in the room. She spoke French elegantly, perhaps better than the French. Catherine received her degrees from Swarthmore and USC. During our term at the Abbey, she accepted a tenure-tracked assistant professorship at MIT. She was a truly brilliant person, intellectually competitive, and extremely interesting to be around. Catherine was married to an American professor who I never met. During the past year, Catherine and her husband moved to Edinburgh, Scotland, where he secured a teaching position. Catherine, a recent doctorate recipient, had found only partial employment in Edinburgh, well beneath her talent. Securing the MIT gig was fantastic for her, but the job brought a new challenge in that she and her husband would most likely live apart, at least for a while.

The French teacher was named Kathy. Kathy was another 26-or-so-year-old young woman with medium length black hair and a sweet, unassuming smile. She was born and raised in Pennsylvania and enrolled at the University of Southern Mississippi, where she was working towards an advanced degree in French. A truly bright spot in Kathy's life was her Spanish boyfriend. He came to visit her in Pontlevoy and she visited him in Spain as she could during class breaks. Kathy's mother and sister also came to visit her in Pontlevoy. The three had a great time, but preparation for the visit was anxiety-inducing for Kathy as she struggled to find adequate lodging and entertainment for her affluent and culturally adroit older sister.

Pamela was the student manager for the first half of the term. She was an ex-pat from New England who lived in Pontlevoy. Pamela was married to Alban, the man who helped me find my rental home. Pamela was creative in a crazy, delightful way. She was fairly tall and very slender, always cheerful, and always smiling. Pamela seemed to wear a different hat each day, usually some form of beret or knit stocking cap brightly colored with patterns of polka dots, flowers, or stripes. Her black tights were covered with long, mismatched and brightly striped stockings pulled up to her knees.

Pamela was an artist. Her creations were intensely abstract, not born from anything found on this planet, but rather from the kinetic energy whirling around inside her head. She was ambidextrous between French and English and was wonderfully adept at connecting the Abbey and its students to the village. Pamela and Alban had one child, Mattice, a fourteen-year-old boy who was a perfect blend between Pamela's sweetness and Alban's charismatic and dark good looks. The three of them lived in a funky, bohemian home that was arranged with full attention to feng shui principles. The rooms were separated by either curtains or rows of beads. The first thing you did when you went into Pamela and Alban's house was to take your shoes off.

Pamela's husband, Alban, was a tall, dark Francophone from North Africa who spoke fluent English. He was a deal-maker who made a living on the fringe of marginally profitable real estate transactions and a home-based film production business. Alban became a good friend, but I learned early on that with Alban there was no free lunch. When thanking him for his assistance in helping me find a home to rent, I unfortunately chose the expression that "there was no way that I could ever repay him."

He corrected me. There was, in fact, a way. Alban hatched a plan involving his purchase of an exotic digital camera, a new technology imbedded into the frame of a pair of dark glasses. The design allowed the photographer to capture action shots hands free. The technology was expensive and not yet available in France. The plan was for Alban to order the camera, have it delivered to my home in the States, and for me to mule it to Alban when I came to Pontlevoy. The plan made me uneasy. I suspected the transaction's basis was most likely a VAT tax dodge and at least a minor customs breach. Also, the camera and its packaging were bulky, consuming a meaningful portion of my precious cargo space. In any event, I owed the debt and followed through smuggling Alban's camera in my bags.

Elizabeth came on to reprieve Pamela as student manager at midterm. This was a planned handoff, as Pamela had some personal matters to which she needed to attend, chiefly preparing to move with her family back to the States later that summer. Pamela and Elizabeth were both wonderful in their student manager roles, but couldn't have been more different.

Pamela was scattered, effusive, and creative. She was constantly looking to develop interesting tours and events for the students (i.e. a local mushroom cave, a winery, a silk worm habitat, and a goat cheese farm). She also coordinated ice breaking activities as the students arrived, arranged for the students to attend local grade school events, and matched every student with a local host family. These connections were awesome for the students, as they allowed them to learn about French culture and what life was like in a small French village.

Pamela's brightest shining moment was her orchestration of a fantastical event she called of "Dinner in the Dark." At Dinner in the Dark, the students sat blindfolded around the vast Abbey dining room table in muted silence, relying just upon their senses of touch, taste, smell, and sound to guide them. After dinner the students performed original plays, sang, and read poetry themed to Leonardo da Vinci. The room was only dimly lit and the mood bizarre, akin to that associated with French mimes.

While artistic expression was Pamela's strength, coordinating complex and detailed things such as purchasing rail passes in mass for the students, arranging hotel accommodations in multiple different cities, and generally coordinating travel logistics for a large group was not.

Elizabeth took over for Pamela at midterm as the students' study travel kicked into gear. For Elizabeth, the details and logistical elements of the student manager position were second nature. She was a 75-year-old longstanding Abbey Program veteran. Unlike Pamela, Elizabeth was detailed-oriented and disciplined. Rules were of utmost import and clearly articulated and enforced. Breaches were not ignored, and as a result, things ran smoothly under Elizabeth's watch.

Elizabeth looked every bit the part of the loving grand matriarch with her short, gray, finally combed hair stored neatly beneath her dark green beret-style stocking cap. Elizabeth was lean and elegant with hazel green eyes. She had traveled France since she was a teenager and has since been forever smitten with the French and their culture. Elizabeth's French, like Pamela's, was exquisite. As I came to know Elizabeth, I wondered why she didn't live in France rather than Hattiesburg, Mississippi. She so adored France. Elizabeth was born and raised in Chicago and came to live in Mississippi only as a result of her now-deceased husband's career. On her own admission Elizabeth admitted that her roots had never grown very deep in Hattiesburg. Her grown daughters lived in New York and Chicago, as did her brother, who is a well-known Broadway playwright. Her annual forays to France, together with her summer visits to her daughters and grandchildren, kept her spirit polished and shining.

Along with the midterm transition of student manager from Pamela to Elizabeth came a few other transitions. Catherine left at midterm and went back to Scotland. Jennifer arrived from Australia. And two other professors, Brian and Jill, joined the program for just two weeks to lead the study groups traveling to Berlin and Rome, respectively.

Brian was a history professor on staff at USM Hattiesburg. His degree was from the University of

Chicago. It was all too appropriate that Brian led the Berlin tour group. He looked every bit the part of a Nazi, albeit a good-natured one. He wore thin wire-rimmed glasses and sported a slight mustache. He adamantly denied that he spoke with a suppressed German accent, but he did. And he would never laugh whenever I asked him, "Comrade, ver are ze papers?"

Jill was an art history professor and at the juncture of taking a new job with Virginia Commonwealth. She had shoulder-length blonde hair and lively blue eyes. The students loved Jill for her joie de vie, her whopping big smile, and her infectious laugh. As much as anything, Jill showed the students the ropes and taught them how to have fun while they traveled, learned, and explored.

And then there were the students. As a group they numbered 26—23 young women and three young men. Most were from Mississippi, a few from Texas, and a small contingent from Wayne State in Detroit. Impressively, seven were Presidential Scholars. As a group they were very accepting of each other and their respective differences. They quickly grew together as one big happy family.

There was a group of half a dozen sorority sisters from Hattiesburg. These sisters were cute, charming, polite, deeply Christian, bright, outgoing, and fun—so much fun. They seemed to have a formal dress or smart outfit for every occasion. They wore makeup at all times and were always well-put-together for public appearance. They were wonderful and wore their southern skin with pride.

Beyond the sorority sisters, there was one young couple who had been dating for three years. They were inseparable. There was one smiling young black woman with dread locks, a former high school basketball player. There was one nice, quiet young woman of Hispanic descent. There was one young girl who was always getting lost or on the verge of it. It didn't take long for us to understand why her mother had sent her to France dressed in a florescent orange jacket and pink pants—beacons to make it easier for us to find her. There was a brilliant young female student from Detroit who went through life producing a slate of straight A+'s. There was a quiet girl from Texas who loved to read and write and who spent all of her spare time rendering exceptional sketchings. There was one huge young man who looked the part of a football lineman until you came to know his gentle, non-athletic personality. There was one small-statured young man who came onto the scene as a quiet film major. As the semester unfolded, it was amazing to watch his transformation into a provocative and worldly ladies' man.

Most of the students partied in good spirits. There were a few who regularly over-imbibed. All of the students took advantage of the opportunity to travel extensively throughout Europe. It's fair to say that all of them experienced important, life-altering transformations during their time at the Abbey. It's also no overstatement to say that they developed close, lasting relationships with each other.

Besides the students and staff, there were a few others I came to know well.

Johan was the Abbey groundskeeper and handyman. Johan was probably in his late twenties with closely cropped hair and wild, but loyal, eyes and a strong, compact build. Johan's mother and father were Pinochets who emigrated from Algeria to France. Coming from Algiers, Johan's French and English dialects were equally difficult to comprehend. His parents were both deceased, which left Johan solely responsible to care for his physically handicapped younger brother. Johan was a kind and helpful person who would do anything he possibly could to be of any assistance—to anyone. He worked the Abbey grounds tirelessly without pay under the trusting belief that the property's owner back in the States would recognize his worth and someday put him on the payroll. His strategy worked, as he gained a paycheck towards the end of our term.

Michael and Susan were expatriates from St. Louis. Retired, Michael and Susan boldly purchased a dilapidated house in Pontlevoy that they were in the process of wonderfully restoring. Michael was a retired IBM executive and a very open, nice man, fond of conversation. Susan was delightful as well. Her mannerisms always reminded me of a Jewish grandmother, boisterous and 100% certain of her opinions and advice. Michael and Susan were both very welcoming to me when we would see each other on the street, and we shared a few memorable meals together.

Phil and Vicky were also ex-pats. They lived in the country just outside Pontlevoy in a charmingly restored former manger. Phil was an avid cyclist and, I was told, related to Jacqueline Onassis.

Bob was an ex-pat born in Ohio who fled Southern California in favor of the Loire Valley a few years ago. Bob was once a film producer, but had to "get out of LA because it was so crazy." For the past few years, despite having no visible means of support, Bob moved happily from home to home, living in them and doing odd fix-up jobs while the owners were away. Bob was a nice and friendly guy who was interested in learning about others. He frequently volunteered to lend his film production skills to support student projects.

Anne Cécile and her family ran the Domaine des Roy, an organic vineyard across the street from the Abbey. Jon Luc owned the area's cheverie. His goat cheese was sublimely artisan, rolled in special ash and skewered in the center with a particular variety of straw to impart flavor. My landlord, Marc, and his partner, Marie, lived in the country between Pontlevoy and Montrichard. Celine was a petite and glamorous ballet dancer from Blois, a friend of Kevin and Jennifer's. Francois and his wife made their living running the village's small Cocci Marché in town. They were both so friendly.

And, of course, there was Julien at Le Commerce, who prepared lunches for the Abbey group every day and who tended bar at night, bringing in traveling bands, streaming soccer matches, and hosting period-themed parties for us. We all became regulars at Le Commerce, partly because it the only show in town, but more because we all very fond of Julien and the welcoming ambiance he hosted at Le Commerce.

All in all, between the students, the staff, and the villagers, Pontlevoy became, for me, a home and a neighborhood in a foreign country. I felt welcome and connected to many people. I was frequently invited to dinner at people's homes. Small parties at Le Commerce, the Abbey, or someone's home often happened spontaneously. I couldn't walk, jog, or bike through the village without seeing someone I knew. In this regard, my experience in Pontlevoy was unlike any other of my life. This was a fertile and unique environment where new experiences and relationships occurred.

And then there was Terry Netter, a man who would come to change my life forever.

Café at Chenonceau—from left to right me, Pamela, Doug, and Kevin

Chapter 8
Terry Netter

As I came to know Terry Netter his life experiences and perspectives arrested me in a way like no one else's I have ever known. While I do not necessarily believe that things happen for a reason, I do believe that important things happen only rarely in one's life and that it is incumbent upon us all to take notice and act upon these important events when they occur. Meeting Terry Netter was an important event for me and I duly took notice.

The first time I met Terry was the night of the Abbey student orientation. With a crowd of mostly strangers gathered around, Doug began lighting up the classroom, exciting the students about the wild, unknown, and unimaginably fantastic life-changing experiences coming their way. Following Doug's animated opening salvo, the students stood up one by one and, in obligatory fashion, provided their names and where they were from. Next, Pamela had invented some weird ice breaking activities and divided the students into pairs to follow along.

Close your eyes. I'm over here! No, here! Now I'm over here! Now run towards the wall as fast as you can. Trust me. I'll yell "Stop!" before you crash against the wall.

The students played along, nervously. Then we went around the room and the professors each took a few moments to introduce themselves. Doug introduced me as his cousin. He took the liberty to position me as a seasoned corporate leader who was going to facilitate a not-for-credit "Leadership Symposium." Doug and I had touched briefly on the matter, but spoke in no detail about me leading a symposium. "We'll figure it out," he'd told me the last time we talked about it a few months back. Doug has a strong tendency towards spontaneity, which was revealing itself now.

On the spot, I stood and explained the symposium. Those who were interested could gather at my house on Sunday nights to work on developing leadership and communication skills. We would learn how to create an inspiring and compelling vision through the art of storytelling. Another subject of focus would be the importance of ethics and how to lead with integrity. Next we would work on coaching skills and the delivery of high impact feedback as well as practicing active listening skills such as the art of asking open ended questions, paraphrasing, and demonstrating empathy. We would concentrate on building self-awareness of our individual talents, strengths, biases, and weaknesses, and on helping others do the same. And finally, it was important that we train ourselves to slow things down and notice both the details and the broad patterns of what's happening and learn how to help others notice and see the broad picture as well. Martha Saunders, the former and recently retired CEO of University of Southern Mississippi, would be joining us for the first session, a big selling point for the students.

I also took a moment to tell the students that I was reading my parents' love letters from World War II. And I promised to find ways to share these correspondences with them, particularly when we travelled to the Normandy beaches later in the term.

As we neared the end of the introductions, an 84-year-old man stood unsteadily to introduce himself. "My name is Terry Netter." He braced himself with a chair and explained that he wasn't feeling well, demonstrating with a tuberculosic cough. His hair was closely cropped, disheveled, and silver. He strongly resembled the elder priest in *The Exorcist*. The man had no hips, creating the persistent possibility that his trousers might fall to the ground. He continued, "I have been associated with the Abbey for a number of years in several capacities. This semester I'll be teaching a course concerning art history and western civilization. I hope you take it. If you do, I hope you will enjoy it." He sat back down, obviously relieved that he was no longer standing.

We made our way around the rest of the room and completed introductions. Later, as we were leaving the room, I approached Professor Netter and introduced myself. For some reason, without advance thought, I blurted a question, "Do you mind if I audit your class?"

He straightened a bit, tilted his head, and smiled. "By all means. Please do...and contribute. It will make the class better."

And that was the beginning. For the students, ice had been broken and introductions had been made. Strangers were on a path towards friendship. Everyone was keen to get the semester going. I was pleased to learn that twelve students immediately signed up for my leadership symposium, causing me to begin for the first time to think through what the symposium might actually sound and feel like.

I also thought casually about the art class I had just signed up to audit. Taking an art class had never occurred to me, ever. My cupboard of artistic talent was as barren as Old Mother Hubbard's. But this was the stuff of which low commitment was made. I told myself that I could always drop the class if I didn't like it. But I had a strange sense that this class was going to be more than just interesting. It was going to be important.

Dogmatic Slumber

I began to know Terry first through the class he taught. Despite the fact that the lingering cold and congestion sapped his strength, it was clear that this was a clever and highly educated man. Terry would lean into his subject matter and also lean across the lectern, both for effect and support as he addressed the class. He struggled valiantly to recall student names, "Desiré? That was the name of Napoleon's fiancée. I'll remember you!" But he would not.

Terry had authored a textbook to facilitate the class, a good one. But he was easily distracted while delivering lectures and often strayed off course. He would roam unpredictably from, say, Chapter 3, to a discussion of what sights to see when visiting the town of Tours, to a historic rendering of the various French kings, and so on, interesting sidebars that only tangentially pertained to the course subject matter. Whenever he was about to veer off road, Terry would head to the white board at the front of the class and begin drawing things to support his detour. It was sometimes hard to tell where Terry was going. That was because he didn't pay close attention to the destination. He was our tour guide and he pointed out spontaneous and unexpected things of interest as we made our way along. It really didn't matter if Terry stayed on subject or not. All of it was interesting.

I got to know Terry personally outside of the classroom. We would often have lunch together at Le Commerce, not just he and I but usually with a small group. He would drive up to the restaurant in his small silver Peugeot and get out wearing his black-on-black

Yankee baseball cap and Ray Charles wrap around shades waving, "How you kids doing?" Then he would shuffle into Le Commerce to eat lunch with us, always with a glass of crisp Rosé.

We would often get together for wonderful meals and picnics at his home or at restaurants in the Valley. I liked Terry. He showed a genuine interest in understanding my renaissance and was eager to hear about the changes I was making in my life. He cheered me on.

The more I learned about Terry's story, the more fascinated I became. It was a strong life's story, in fact one that was written up by *Life Magazine* back in 1968. Two of the most interesting, most defining aspects of Terry's story were clearly at odds with one other. First, he was an artist, a very good one. Second, he was a Jesuit priest, a former one. That Terry would choose to enter the priesthood made for an interesting story. That he would later choose to leave it doubled down on the drama that has unfolded as his life.

Terry grew up during the Depression near Bronxville, an affluent northern suburb of New York City. His father was an executive with Paramount Pictures, his mother a stage performer who once danced with Ginger Rogers. His mother was Roman Catholic. His father was Jewish, before converting to Catholicism. Terry's mannerisms and voice intonations are reminiscent of New York Jewish cadence, which I presume is largely attributable to his father and growing up in and around New York.

Terry was the youngest of four boys. His brothers were athletic, charismatic, and successful business types. Terry was charismatic but not athletic. And he was no business type. He wanted most to be an artist. He was gifted in this area, but neither his parents nor his teachers nurtured this talent as a respectable profession for him to pursue.

Although Terry grew up a Catholic, the household was far from pious. As a youngster, Terry viewed priests as esteemed leaders in the church and in the community. Compared to others they seemed to Terry to be mostly loving, happy, and kind. It was as a senior in high school that Terry first thought about becoming a priest and then rather abruptly decided that he would do just that. His decision was a surprise to his parents, his friends, and in a way even to himself. He entered the vocation, never looking back.

Until I met Terry it never occurred to me what it meant to be a Jesuit. My limited awareness was built upon on vague knowledge that Jesuits were men who, for some inexplicable reason, had taken vows to divest themselves of all property, to blindly obey the Pope, and to be celibate. And, true, this is how things are for a Jesuit. However, the other side of the coin is that the Jesuit path is an incredible scholastic journey. The Jesuits study history, philosophy, theology, and language in an intensely devoted and meditative manner. It is a rigorously unrivaled path of formal education.

Terry spent over twenty years as a Jesuit, beginning with the novitiate and culminating with ordination. The

Jesuits afforded Terry a remarkable education, an English BA and a Philosophy MA from Fordham University, an LST in Theology from the University of Innsbruck, and an MFA from George Washington University. He is fluent in German, French, and English. He passed the incredibly difficult Ad Grad, a grueling two-hour oral examination before a panel of church scholars entirely in Latin. And he studied under one of the great theologians of our time, Karl Rahner.

All along the way, Terry maintained his strong desire to be an artist. Over the years he continually petitioned his seniors to allow him to pursue his love for art. Time and time again he was rebuked, until finally a kind Provincial relented. Terry was granted permission to pursue an advanced art degree through George Washington University. That the Jesuits allowed him to purse a graduate art degree rather than the traditionally accepted paths such as history, theology, or philosophy was an extraordinary and, in fact, unheard of exception. Terry dove in head first, studying art, art history, and perfecting his craft as an artist. Through his work in the classroom and his artistic creations, he gained widespread acclaim. He became known as the Priest Who Paints.

Terry's art has been exhibited around the world. His paintings are unique and his style constantly evolving. His most recent works are colorful Zen landscapes set in the French countryside with a meditative focus on a low horizon, usually with a full sky opening to the heavens. His works have attracted a loyal following of patrons who come to Long Island each fall to buy and collect the paintings that Terry created the previous spring in France.

Terry's life as a Jesuit took an abrupt and unexpected turn one day during the fall of 1966. He was in New York with one of his brothers, walking in Central Park when they ran into an acquaintance. She was a beautiful and charming young woman, Therese Franzese, the sister of a former student. They greeted each other, exchanged pleasantries, and discussed meeting up again. From that chance encounter, Terry and Therese kindled an unintended relationship. Their relationship was platonic, but they were beginning to have strong feelings towards each other. Pursuing things further was not possible given Terry's vows of celibacy and obedience. Their relationship could not exist under the Church's rules. They broke it off.

Separated from Therese, Terry began to harbor doubt. Was their separation the right thing? Why so? Other serious doubts about his role as a Jesuit began to creep in as well. Terry was having difficulty carrying the party line regarding homosexuality. Why would a loving god exclude persons on this basis? The Church's prioritization of men over women and views on birth control were troubling to him as well. Times were changing; at least in Terry's mind, the Institutional Roman Catholic Church was not adapting. The institution of the church was both out of touch and unreasonable with respect to these issues. Terry's belief in God was based on the premise that God was a loving God, accessible to all individuals through many paths. This belief was difficult to mesh with the Vatican's tight control over the access to God and its very stringent stance with respect to personal interpretations of God.

Terry awoke one day with a dramatic change of heart, one that would mark a turning point in his life. He called Therese. He wanted to talk. And what a talk it was. Terry explained to Therese that he could easily continue to accept his vow of poverty, but that he could no longer abide by his vow of obedience to the Pope. More importantly, he also could no longer live with his vow of celibacy.

"I plan to petition the Pope to release me from my vows. I love you! Will you marry me?" he cried.

Her response was unsettling. Therese laughed, almost uncontrollably.

"What? What are you laughing at?" he asked.

"It's funny! I've been thinking the same thing," she said as her laughter turned to tears, tears both of joy and fear of the unknown. What lay ahead for the two of them?

Terry followed through with his request to be released from his vows, which the Pope granted. He and Therese married and have shared a great loving life together from that point on. They had a son, Dylan, who is grown and teaches in Miramar. Together, Terry and Teresa have travelled the world. They have a home on Long Island and a beautiful country home near St. George-Sur-Cher, not far from Pontlevoy. The home in St. George is surrounded by woods, flowering shade trees, and a thicket of bamboo. A small, clear stream flows nearby. The country smells of St. George are vividly French, as are the sounds. Soft cuckoo and pheasant calls roll across the fields and out from the woods, mixing with the sweet aroma of cherry blossoms. Here in the French countryside, Terry gathers his inspiration to paint.

Despite formally leaving his position with the Church, Terry still considers himself to be a priest, albeit an inactive one. He also still considers himself a Catholic, but no longer a member of the Institutional Roman Catholic Church. He often refers to himself as a Transdenominational Christian with Catholic roots. However one says it, Terry has sustained a heartfelt faith in God, a faith that he readily admits flies in the face of all reason. Terry credits the Jesuits with giving him the intellectual tools to both work his way out of the Institutional Roman Catholic Faith as well as to find his way back to a strong personal faith. His faith transcends his entire being.

After class one day, Terry asked me directly if I believed in God. He may have asked me if I was a Christian. I don't recall. I answered that I did not, that I was unchurched. He readily accepted that and candidly discussed his doubt as well.

He certainly had no interest in converting or convincing me. At the same time he spoke openly about his choice to believe. Terry believed in God and he believed in prayer. He prayed often, almost always beginning with the phrase, "Dear God, if there is a God." He confided to me that Therese hates it when he does that. Terry also often referred to God as "she" or "her," reflecting an unwillingness to presume God's sex. Likewise, he maintained firm conviction that men and women are equal both in life and in God's eyes.

As I came to know Terry better over time, I came to appreciate his scholarly background and his ability to understand the world around us, to fill in important aspects of the world that, for most of us, are unseen or not understood. Terry was able to notice moments, events, and occurrences and uniquely able to understand them in the context of well-reasoned connections. For instance, the class Terry taught was not really the art class I had expected. Rather, the curriculum followed a broad sweeping evolutionary tract of history, religion, and philosophy and how those evolutions have been reflected in art and the creative process through the ages.

The class dialogue began with the ancient Greeks, moved to the Medieval Ages, then on to the Renaissance, and concluded with the impressionistic and modern art eras. We discussed Socrates, Plato, and Aristotle. We studied art imitating nature, Plato's *Demiurge*, *The Republic*, and Aristotle's *Theory of Metaphysics* and the essence of reality.

With great relish, Terry harpooned me in front of the class as he stepped through the three classes of Plato's *Republic*: philosophers, military, and mercantile. Here he paused and described in more detail the mercantile, the lowest class, populated with people such as *bankers*. He sneered as he said the word *banker*, scrunching up his face as though there were some sort of terrible stench in the room. He looked at me and wrung his hands as if they needed to be washed. It was all in good fun. And I was vindicated as the course progressed. In the end, Terry was forced to concede my occupation's contribution to the arts as evidenced by powerful banking families such as the Medici, Rothschild, Mellon, and Rockefeller families—all great patrons of the arts.

The class transitioned from the Greeks, who felt that the role of art was to imitate nature, to Alexander the Great and the Roman Empire. We discussed the rise of Christianity, when art assumed a new role, the role of helping man envision the unseen world of grace. We talked about Constantine, Charlemagne, and the Dark Ages. We talked about St. Thomas Aquinas and his beatific vision and faith-seeking reason. We studied the exquisitely refined art of the Renaissance: Michelangelo, Raphael, Botticelli, and the master, da Vinci. We pressed on, moving through history: Rembrandt, the Baroque, and Rococo periods. We studied the religious wars that resulted from the bitter split between the Protestants and the Catholics and how those variations on the same faith approached art differently. The Catholics essentially employed art as a propaganda tool used to recruit and retain members to the church. The Protestants, by contrast, used art to celebrate the individual and the individual's spiritual relationship with God.

We studied Galileo, Copernicus, and Descartes. And, because we were in France, we took advantage of that fact and spent quite a bit time discussing the French kings and the quirkiness of their respective reigns. Then we moved on to the Age of Enlightenment—Hume, Kant, and Hegel—which brought us to modern day art, theology, and philosophy.

I found the subject matter, the study of art, interesting. I found the connection of man's evolving relationship with God to the creative process enlightening. I found the man teaching the class fascinating. Terry and I became close friends. I was open about my agnostic views. And I listened with interest as he spoke about his views. I was receptive to learning about Terry's convictions in a way that would not have been possible if Terry were a zealot. Terry was anything but that. He did talk openly about his faith, but he readily admitted, "It's insane. It makes no sense."

He would tell me how he prayed regularly. Prayer was contrary to any logical thought process. And yet he believed that prayer worked. Terry did not believe that God would intervene to override the laws of nature. But he believed that prayer somehow made a difference. He also readily acknowledged his doubt, the uncertainty of God's existence. How could anyone know for sure? Faith has to defy reason. Those who claim to be certain, who claim to be "right," cannot be. Doubt is a fundamental aspect of faith.

These perspectives from a highly educated man, a man who was as deeply emerged in faith as a soul could be, a man who had reasoned his way out of a lifelong devotion to the Institutional Roman Catholic Church, a man who openly acknowledged doubt, were delivered with a level of integrity and objectiveness that I had never before encountered.

Terry's class lasted for six weeks, and my attentiveness grew as we went along. It was during the last day of class when we came to Immanuel Kant. That was when things really came together for me. Terry had continued teaching the class despite being nearly gravely ill for the duration. He was losing strength and barely had enough as he walked unsteadily into the room to begin the day's lecture. He took a deep breath, wiped his nose, and coughed into his handkerchief as he warned the class to, "Buckle your seat belts. It's about to get interesting!"

At that point, I felt as if all of this man's strength and purpose were directed exclusively towards me. The class was culminating in this moment and Terry and I were the only ones in the room. That's how it felt, and Terry would later acknowledge that to be the case. His remarks were directed at me. I hung on his every word.

Kant's three related books, *The Critique of Pure Reason*, *The Critique of Practical Reason*, and *The Critique of Judgment* made perfect sense to me. The last book of the three, *The Critique of Judgment*, was most germane to the class since it dealt primarily with art and aesthetic judgments. The other two books, however, were the most pertinent to me personally. Kant reasons in *The Critique of Pure Reason* that God's existence cannot logically be derived. Reason is limited to phenomena that can be observed. God cannot be observed; ergo God does not exist in the world of reason. But Kant does not stop there. *The Critique of Practical Reason* carries the discussion further by putting forth three postulates: 1) Man has the freedom to act; 2) Man is guided by a moral compass—the concepts of good and evil come to us from somewhere; and 3) There must be someone or something after life to mete out justice to those who choose to do evil rather than good acts.

These postulates may or may not be true. But in Kant's view, these were moral postulates that can neither be proven nor discredited. From the perspective of these postulates, God has to exist, not as an object of reason but as an object of faith. Something—God—has instilled the sense of good and evil within us. We know the difference. And at the end of the day, God stands ready to render justice against evil acts. The belief in God, according to Kant, is a moral choice rather than an intellectual act, since God is not an observable phenomenon.

Hegel picked up where Kant left off. Hegel viewed humankind in terms of our evolution. Tying that back to the creative process, art becomes a product of the times in which it is created. Hegel coined the term "zeitgeist," or the spirit of the times in which we live. The art of the dark ages was a product of the zeitgeist at the time, as was the art created during the impressionistic era, as was the art of the modern era, and so on. Collectively, mankind has an evolved consciousness, a consciousness that is building upon itself...and for what purpose? According to Teilhard de Chardin, a noted French philosopher and Jesuit priest, perhaps the purpose is unknown to us, but perhaps together we are all building and advancing towards an Omega Point that is God's plan.

As the class wrapped up, I reflected on what I had learned—a lot. That said, nothing in particular had changed. I found the history, the art, the philosophy, and the theology all very interesting, but not in a way that signified anything especially noteworthy or life-changing. And yet, in another way, I found myself soaking on things. I was paying attention to the world around me in a way that I never had before. I was only vaguely aware, if at all, that something was bubbling up into my consciousness, something important, something that I would want to notice.

Lunch at Terry Netter's home. Left to right: Ben, Terry (standing), Dave, Catherine, and Kevin (foreground)

"Yearning" by Terence Netter

Chapter 9
Life in the Loire

Life in the Loire quickly grew comfortable for me the more I became acquainted with its people and the more I became familiar with my surroundings. Francois's Cocci Marché in Pontlevoy was a short walk for day-to-day grocery staples, as was the boulangerie. Once a week or so I would drive to the Super U in Montrichard for more varied and extensive grocery selections.

My French was "pas très belle," but over time I became increasingly able to comprehend others and to communicate my intent. A milestone was my trip to the Darty (France's answer to Best Buy) store near Blois to buy a wireless extender, the diagnosed solution to my home's faint Wi-Fi connection. Finding the store in the suburban maze of Blois was a challenge. Describing my problem in French (how to boost an internet connection originating from the other side of a three-foot-thick stone wall) was a greater hurdle yet. However, to my grand satisfaction, I was able to make myself understood. The floor attendant and I agreed on his recommended solution, and voila! For the reasonable sum of 60€ the problem was solved.

This initiative was no insignificant thing. By the grace of the Wi-Fi extender, I was now able to check email, communicate via Facebook, visit with Laura, Audrey, and Will through Skype, listen to music, and stream sporting events such as the Super Bowl, Iowa Hawkeye basketball games, and Champions League soccer matches.

With the Darty/Wi-Fi success in hand, I was faced with another formidable linguistic challenge—dinner with my landlord, Marc, and his partner, Marie. This was a two-hour ordeal entirely in French. I grabbed every single word from my shelf of French vocabulary and put them to use—not always good use, but to use nonetheless.

"Your dogs are very pretty. What do you call them? They are black and white, yes?"

"I like France. It is good, no, beautiful!"

"I ride my bike today. Downhill to Bourée, whee! Very fast! Uphill to Pontlevoy, whew! Very difficult! I am tired."

"How do you like Obama? Good or bad?"

"Dinner is very good! Thank you very much!"

"Good night, my friends!"

And so it went. I managed to come away with a victorious spirit, the elation I would get whenever it was realized that my French was better than the other person's English. It was at these moments when the other person and I would spontaneously agree to use French "entre nous." True, it was a bit awkward when I hugged and kissed both Marie (appropriate) and Marc (not) as we said goodbye. I guess I was just caught up in the moment.

I drove back to town, exhausted from the conversational effort. However, I wasn't done with my French for the evening just yet. I drove, my headlights piercing just the few feet of darkness directly in front of my car. As I approached the first dim street light of Pontlevoy, I could scarcely make out an image that didn't belong. Something wasn't right. What was it? Oh my god!

It was a young woman running out of the shadows towards my car. What caught my eye was the lengthy stream of fabric from her dark red shawl. Her long, wavy brown hair flowed backwards from the velocity of her frantic dash. As I drew near, I could see her eyes, wild and panicked.

"Appellez la Policia! Appellez la Policia!" she screamed not once, not twice, but repeatedly.

She had come from the shadowed side of the road. I looked over and glimpsed the silhouette of a man. He appeared to be wielding a knife, or at least some object that I construed to be a weapon. He was a ways away but walking towards us. I braked quickly and opened the passenger door. "Dans la voiture, mamemoisel! Maintenant! Vit! Vit!" (Get in the car! Now! Quickly!)

She jumped into the car and closed the door, falling back into the passenger seat. I looked at her face. She was striking. She wore scarlet red lipstick. Her eyes were wild and she was breathless, unable to tell me anything about the situation. She held a cell phone and frantically punched at its buttons, over and over again. Who was she trying to call? The police? She didn't say.

I came to a stop 100 yards down the road and tried to speak to her. I asked what had happened ("Ce qui s'est passé?"). She wouldn't say. I told her as best I could that I didn't speak much French, but that she was safe. I would help her ("Je vous aidez!"). But before I could complete the gyrations of these words, she suddenly leapt out of the car and fled.

I couldn't just leave her there. I drove around the block searching. There! There she was in a phone booth. An alarmed woman from a nearby home peaked out of a half-opened door before it quickly slammed shut. I persuaded the frightened woman to get back in my car and convinced her that I would take her to safety. I tried to calm her without much affect. "Où voulez-vous allez?" (Where do you want to go?)

She told me, "Une Place du College." I knew this address. Puzzling. It was the Abbey's. I drove the few blocks to the Abbey front gate and slowed as we approached. Before the car could come to rest, she flung open the door and jumped out. She ran towards an apartment building adjacent to Le Commerce and disappeared into the darkness of an open swinging door.

And that's where my story ends. I don't know what was at the root of her panic, nor do I know what became of her. I never saw her again. I did stop by Le Commerce that night to let Julien know what had just happened. He frowned as I told him the story. He told me that this young woman and her male companion were strangers to town, recent and transient tenants of the apartment next door. They were known to fight with each other. He suspected drug use. Julien told me that late last night, just before closing, the man had accosted patrons at Le Commerce. Half out of this mind, the man pulled a knife and nicked Julien in a fleeting scuffle before turning to leave. I did not see or hear any more about this dangerously matched couple. But their story and their future remained on my mind, a mystery with an unknown, but likely unpleasant, ending.

This unsettling occurrence was out of character for Pontlevoy. (Well there was also the night that the band of Romas came to Le Commerce and began breaking beer bottles. They were looking for a fight, but the gendarmes came to take them away before they could find one. But that was an exception to the norm as well.)

Overall, I was having a grand time. I attended Terry's classes daily and was being drawn into what I was learning from him. I was also greatly enjoying my Leadership Symposium meetings on Sunday evenings. And every week there seemed to be something new and interesting to do or see.

Early in the semester Julien hosted a Mardi Gras party at Le Commerce, complete with costumes for all. My costume was a simple one, a mask with beads. Others were more elaborate. Julien crafted an incredibly fierce devil costume, replete with red face paint, glowing red contact lenses, fangs, and a pointed tail flowing from his black tights. Keenon got first prize, in my book. He came as Louis XIV, wearing purple tights and a faux leopard-spotted shawl, holding a scepter, and adorned with a crown perched atop a wig of long flowing locks. Infatuated with Louis XVI's narcissistic personae, Keenon played it well. He thoroughly embraced the personality of the sun god and, at least for one night, the entire world did in fact seem to revolve around him. It was hysterical to watch this character come to life in the form of this flamboyant, young black man from Mississippi.

Julien regularly hired regional bands to play at Le Commerce. The bands were average at best, but brought great fun to the brasserie's small dance floor as they played stale American hits or European pop songs. The students loved line dancing to the live bands or, absent a live band, dancing to Julien's DJ repertoire. They hollered loudly whenever their theme song came on, "Sweet Home Alabama."

There were also dinner gatherings, at Pamela and Alban's, at Doug's prior to his return to the states, at Terry's country home, at Mike and Susan's, at Kevin and Jennifer's, or at chez moi. There were many great local restaurants: Le Precopia in Montrichard (moules frites!), Le Bousquet set in a cave out in the country (biftek with frites and homemade ginger rum!), Le

Biguenée in St. Aignon (frommage crêpes!), L'Auberge de L'École in Pontlevoy (gourmet French—skate wing with bacon-wrapped quail eggs!), La Brazza in Pontlevoy (coffee shop with incredible fruits de mer pizza!), Turkish Délice in Blois (succulent döner sandwiches and kabobs!), and L'Orangerie at Chenenceau (best food in the Valley and a room with a view!). There were many restaurants, but my favorite was Le Guerre in Montrichard, where I learned that the best, most affordable food in France is often right in front of your nose at the train station.

While I was wining and dining in great style, I also greatly anticipated any and all opportunities to stay in touch with my family, to see how they were doing, and to describe what I was up to. Skype worked quite well thanks to my Darty internet booster. Usually I would make appointments with Laura, Audrey, or Will once a week to check in, taking into account time zone differences. I always got a bump talking to them and learning what had happened to them and sharing what had happened to me that day or that week.

The weather during January, February, and March was mostly wintery for sure. My home and the Abbey were both centuries old, with drafty windows and leaky doors, cold stone walls, icy tile floors, and heating systems overmatched by the challenge of heating the space. The occasional light snow showers were beautiful and particularly wondrous to the students from Mississippi and Texas. Rain or shine, I jogged on a nearly daily basis following the circular route I had charted through the village streets and out to the periphery of the countryside.

My greatest pleasure, however, was riding the banged-up old road bike that I borrowed from two avid bikers from Pontlevoy. Pamela introduced me to them when I arrived in Pontlevoy, thinking that they might know where I could rent a bike for my extended stay. Marie Jo and Bernard welcomed me and Pamela to their home one night, where, in my best French (augmented by Pamela's excellent French), I explained my love for biking. I asked about renting a bike. It was only though Pamela's interpretation that I learned the wonderful news. Everyone was smiling but me. But I began smiling broadly as well when Pamela explained the conversation. Bernard had a spare bike that he would gladly lend me. This kind act made all the difference.

With a bike, I was able to explore all of the countryside along and between the Cher and Loire Rivers. I rode several times each week, more often than not bundled for the elements, but sometimes in shirtsleeves as spring progressed. Every ride was the genesis of a glorious day. I loved to explore the region's back roads, mostly single lanes with little or no car traffic. A typical ride would range anywhere from 50 to 100 kilometers through vineyards, across green fields teeming with smarms of brightly colored flowers, and into bucolic neighboring villages: Candé sur Beuvron, Chaumont, St. Aignon, Amboise, Chenonceau, Bourré, Chisseaux, Monthou-Sur-Cher, Céré-la-Ronde, Fresnes, Sambin, Onzaine, St Denis-Sur-Loire, and many more.

Every village had a farmer's market, each on different days of the week. I loved to pedal to the different village markets, all small and friendly. It was easy to talk to the vendors about what was most fresh. And it was rewarding to bike back home loaded with fresh vegetables, fruits, cheeses, sausages, pâtés, and mushrooms. The smell of rotisserie chickens, skewered and roasting, turning slowly, juices dripping below onto a tray of potatoes seasoned with garlic and Herbs de Provence is now Prustian for me. Those aromas will forever instantly return me to the remembrance of the simple and vibrant life I sampled in the Loire.

During my bike rides, fresh, palpable layers of remarkable history came to life, thick layers going back to the ancient Gael and Roman times, the Dark Ages, the Renaissance, the era of French Kings who ruled the world, and the World Wars, both of which were fought here in the gut of France. Each bike ride would take me past a grand chateau, a magnificent cathedral, or a sobering World War I or World War II battle sight.

Just outside of Pontlevoy was La Pierre de Minuit, an ancient Gallic Druid rock formation, thousands of years old. Roman ruins were scattered along the Cher between Bourré and Thésée. Troglodyte homes were endearingly built into cave walls high on the cliffs overlooking the Cher. The Place de Plumereau, set in an enchanting bricked hollow in Tours, was a sea of outdoor restaurants, pubs, and brasseries that bustled at night. The sites were varied and captivating.

The Chateaux in the Loire were likewise both visually stunning and historically fascinating. I biked to all of them—Chenonceau, Cheverny, Blois, Amboise, Chaumont, Loches, Poupon, and more.

Chateau de Chenonceau was my favorite. Built on a bridge, Chenonceau spanned the Cher. It looked like Cinderella's castle, with the spectacular added effect that one could look out its windows and see the river flowing around and beneath the building. The gardens were extensive and finely groomed. The history of things that happened inside Chenonceau was filled with intrigue. Henry II sheltered his mistress, Diane de Poitier, there; Henry died in an unfortunate jousting accident; Henry's wife, Catherine de Medici, put her foot down, evicted Diane, and moved in; Catherine died and gifted Chenonceau to her daughter-in-law, Louise de Lorraine-Vaudemont; Louise's husband, Henry III, was assassinated; Louis painted her bedroom pitch black and spent the rest of her days wandering Chenonceau in ghostlike mourning. In more recent times, Chenonceau served as a hospital during WWI and as a designated prisoner exchange point during WWII.

Chateau de Chaumont, perched majestically overlooking the Loire River, had the most majestic vista of all the Chateaux. Catherine de Medici showed her kinder side to Diane when she evicted her from Chenonceau but relocated her and allowed her to take up residence at Chaumont.

Chateau de Blois was another of Catherine de Medici's favorites. She may have shown her kinder side to Diane, but she left no doubt that her heart was more black than kind the morning she invited the Duc de Guise to breakfast at Blois. Catherine was in a desperate struggle to retain control over France, and the Duc posed a threat. Upon her order, Catherine's guards swarmed the Duc as he entered the dining area for breakfast. They stabbed him repeatedly, sending him to his death. Thus began an era of bloody violence between the Catholics and the Protestants. Catherine would go on to poison many of her perceived enemies and ultimately order the St. Bartholomew Massacre, a heinous but failed attempt to squelch the Protestant movement.

Chateau de Blois also contained one of France's most mind-bending architectural creations, Leonardo de Vinci's four-story, double-helix staircase. It was a work of pure genius. One person can stand at the bottom of the staircase walking up while another person stands at the top walking down. They will never pass each other.

Chateau de Chambord was the most enormous of the Loire Chateaux. Never completed, Chambord was designed on the grandest of scales, stunningly overbuilt with more than 440 rooms and 282 fireplaces. Chambord also contained a second da Vinci staircase similar to the one at Blois.

Chateau de Cheverny was home to the cartoon character Tin Tin. In real life, the Chateau is still home to the Marquis de Vibraye. Cheverny has been in the Marquis's family for more than 600 years. During WWII, the French stashed the Mona Lisa in the family basement to hide it from the Nazis. The Marquis is a direct descendent of Gueldon de Chaumont, the knight who returned from the Crusades to build the Abbey in Pontlevoy. I had the chance to meet the Marquis personally a few years ago when he hosted a Mackaman family gathering coordinated by Doug. Doug and I also got to play a round of golf on his semi-private golf course. Cheverny is surrounded by an immense forest where the Marquis and his pack of hounds hunt boar and stag on horseback. The public feeding of the hounds is a gluttonous frenzy of raw meat.

The Chateau, Don Jon, and Keep of Loches were full of history. Jean d'Arc came to Loches, her objective to persuade Charles VII to travel to Reims to be coronated King of France. This proposal was a dangerous venture, but an important unifying act for France given the divisive circumstance of the time. The Don Jon at Loches was separate from the Chateau and rose hundreds of feet in a tight, vertigo-inducing space. The fortified citizens of Loches would retreat within the protection of the Don Jon's walls to withstand the many lengthy sieges waged against them. The adjacent Keep at Loches was where prisoners were housed and usually tortured before their deaths.

Amboise was where Charles VII brought Leonardo da Vinci to live out his final years. Leonardo toted the Mona Lisa as he rode to Amboise on a donkey. His home, Clos de Lucé, was open to the public. I stood next to the bed where da Vinci died with Charles holding his hand. (Parenthetically, Mick Jagger has a home in Amboise which tends to put all on guard looking and hoping for a Sir Mick encounter. I didn't have one.)

The rich history of the Loire Chateaux was augmented by the more recent history of both World Wars in the Loire. As I biked, I would stop at each village to view their World War I monuments, which were generally situated prominently near Centre Ville. Each monument was, in its own, right moving, testament to the brutality of World War I and the indelible scar that the war left on France.

And then there was World War II or, as some would say, the second half of World War I. The Cher stood as the line of demarcation between occupied and unoccupied France. I always paused as I crossed the Cher to observe the imagined sensation of what it felt like to live in occupied France, to not be allowed to cross the river, to have your country torn in two, and to live each day under the German army's aggressive suppression. There was a pub, Le Passeur, which was situated on the unoccupied bank of the Cher across the river opposite Montrichard. La Passeur was the meeting place where a few brave villagers, at risk of being killed by the Germans or the Vichy, would ferry resistance fighters across the Cher in the dark of night.

The bravery of the resistance fighters was made ever so clear when Catherine and I drove with a few students to the haunting village of Oradour-sur-Glane. Oradour is situated in a pastoral setting, but one which will forever be remembered (souviens toi) for what transpired the morning of June 10, 1944, D-Day plus four. At the time, the resistance movement was strengthening while the Germans were just beginning to lose their grip on France.

A German military leader had been kidnapped near Oradour and purportedly held captive by the resistance. In retribution a German SS troop paused at Oradour on its way from Southern France to Normandy. The Germans circled the village, closed in upon the villagers, directed the women and children to the village church, separated the men into four different buildings, and held them all captive. At high noon, the German commander fired a single shot, which signified the beginning. The soldiers began systematically massacring all 642 people—men, women, and children—with machine gun fire, explosives, and accelerants. There were a few souls who somehow escaped the roundup. But none survived the massacre.

Afterward, the Germans looted what they wanted and destroyed all that they could. From that moment until today, time has stood still in Oradour. Every car was left exactly where it was, rusted and abandoned. Every bicycle, every plundered home and business, every telephone receiver, table, chair, oven, gas pump, and sewing machine has been left exposed to the elements and decaying, a lasting memorial to the dreadful atrocity of that day.

So sad—not angry, just deeply saddened—that's how I felt as I witnessed the remains of the horror that was Oradour. I recoiled as I touched the deep bullet pockmarks on the church walls. I couldn't help myself. I gasped. I could hear the screams as though the murdered souls were still alive. I could feel the reverberations, the rapid and thunderous *bang, bang, bang* of the machine guns as if they were still firing into the terrified crowd. I could make out the hollow, tinny sound of bullet casings dropping and scattering on the floor. And I thought deeply and sadly about the men squeezing the triggers. What could they have been thinking? How on Earth did they decide that this was the right thing to do?

The truth was that massacres like the one at Oradour happened throughout France. But, unlike most, the massacre at Oradour has been timelessly preserved and the cruelty of that day is forever indelibly on display. Oradour has been preserved so that we can all forgive, but not forget, how men can act at their worst. As a man stands over a young girl and pulls the trigger that launches a series of thunderous bullets into her skull and gut, what must he be thinking? We know that he had a mother. Does he believe in God? Surely some of those that pulled the trigger did. If he were facing that God, how would he explain what he did that day? What would he tell his mother?

Several weeks after visiting Oradour, I attended a small but unforgettable dinner party at L'Auberge de L'École, Pontlevoy's most elegant dining establishment. I and my friends, Kevin and Elizabeth, hosted the event for two French nationals, Maurice and Genevieve. The two had travelled to Pontlevoy to address the students the next day. Maurice was a death camp survivor. Genevieve's now-deceased husband was heavily involved with the resistance. She was not formally part of the resistance, but she experienced the war as a young girl placed in extraordinary circumstance.

Maurice, a Jew from Paris, was separated from his family as a young boy and taken to Auschwitz. Now an elderly man, Maurice was tall, slumped with age, and had dark, permanent bags of sorrow beneath his eyes. He spoke English with a heavy accent, but in a soft, muted voice. Maurice described vividly what it felt like to live in Paris as the war came down around him and as his own countrymen conspired with the German forces to round up his family and friends for deportation. Maurice was very articulate and clear. Life in the death camp was misery, but it never occurred to him that he might die there. No one in the camp had any idea of what was happening beyond the drudgery of daily factory work. He saw no one die. He was completely unaware of the gas chambers, the mass burials, the exterminations occurring nearby. He never saw any of this. It was only upon his release from Auschwitz that he became aware. It was only then, when he returned home, that he learned that his mother, father, and brother had all been killed. Without his knowing it, he had seen them for the last time. He no longer had a home. He no longer had a family.

Genevieve was a short, neatly dressed, older woman—very quiet, almost shy. She was unaccustomed to telling stories and clearly uneasy being the center of attention. She smiled slightly as she spoke in French.

She told us how, as a young girl, she'd had a job at her school. Every school in France was required to prominently hang a picture of Marshal Pétain. The picture of Pétain in her school was two-sided. On one side was Pétain. On the other side was a picture of Jesus Christ. Genevieve's job was to quickly turn the picture to the Pétain side whenever the German or Vichy officials came to visit, and to turn it back to the Jesus side after they had left.

She told another story of when she was a young girl. The Germans had invaded and were occupying her village. One day she was swimming with her friends at the public swimming pool. Three severe-looking German soldiers were standing by monitoring things. It was a hot day and the Germans ordered everyone out of the pool so that they could swim. One of the Germans, an officer, stood guard while the other two swam. Genevieve, in a mischievous moment, convinced one of her friends to run playfully in circles around the officer as he stood guard. Cloaked as childish play, but in what actually represented a brave and defiant act, Genevieve bumped into the officer knocking him—gun, uniform and all—into the pool. She laughed telling that story so many years later. I could visualize the angry German officer shouting at her and ordering her from the area, his Nazi cap floating impotently on the surface of the pool.

One of the nuns from school witnessed the commotion at the pool and called Genevieve into her office the next day. The nun spoke, "I know that you are on our side and that you are a girl that can be trusted. I have a secret that I am about to share with you. But before I do, I need to know that you will never share this secret with anybody—not your mother, not your father, not anybody. Do you promise? This is very, very important." Genevieve nodded solemnly and, in fact, kept this secret safe until many, many years after the war, telling no one, not even her parents.

The nun explained that there were two children, a young Jewish boy and girl, who were hidden beneath a trapdoor in the church's floorboards. The nun was giving Genevieve a very important job, to deliver food to the boy and girl each day. "Your job is to feed them and to keep them alive. Remember, this is a secret. Tell no one! Their lives depend upon it." Genevieve took on this responsibility, an enormous one for anyone, let alone a young girl. Dutifully, she brought the children food each day. On her own initiative she also stole candles from the church and gave them to the children to light their tiny crawl space at night. At confession one day, Genevieve told to her priest that she had been stealing candles from the church. She was sorry, but she wasn't able to explain why she was stealing. The Priest acknowledged the theft with a quiet, "I know."

Genevieve never saw the Jewish children directly, only their dark, hidden eyes in the crawlspace. She never spoke a word to them, as she was directed not to. And she never knew what became of them. I suppose similar stories could be told by many, at least by some of those that are still alive. But Genevieve's stories were, to me, brave, sad, and inspiring. They made me cry.

Chenonceau

Cheverny

Double helix staircase at Blois

Chateau Amboise

Chaumont-sur-Loire

Chambourd

Line of Demarcation—Cher at St. Aignon

Oradour-sur-Glane

Dogmatic Slumber

Sidewalk lunch at St. Aignon

Students on the way to Candé-sur-Beuvron

Rapeseed near Céré-la-Ronde

La Bièvre near Fresnes

Mill near Ouchamps

Biking

Mardi Gras at Le Commerce—with Keenon as Louis XVI

Julien at Mardi Gras—Le Commer

Chapter 10
What Happened in WWII Today?

I began reading my parents' love letters as I flew across the Atlantic. I continued reading them during my time in Pontlevoy. The more I read, the more I was drawn into the story. These two characters, passionate lovers separated by the war, were frightened, depressed, witty, and articulate, not my mother or father as I knew them. These people were fascinating, their situation unbearable.

Married nine months, and just 23 years old, my father was shipped worlds away from his young wife. He was farther away than he could have ever imagined from the things he cared most about. An inexperienced captain of an LCT landing craft, he was heading towards grave danger. His crew was mostly young boys, some just 18 years old. Together they would face the most dangerous of situations—beach landings in Italy, North Africa, and Normandy.

My mother's letters were somewhat banal. What was going on back home wasn't very exciting to write about. All she could do was to send love and support to her husband. She did with all her might. Time passed painfully and slowly for her.

My father's letters were much more interesting. His letters told an absorbing story. They spoke to the details of life during the war through his eyes. His words brought to life what it felt like to be in the moment during that endless string of perilous moments.

As I read along, I encountered people during my daily routine in Pontlevoy. I began to tell them about what happened in the batch of letters I had most recently read. It became a regular question that others would ask: "So, what happened today in World War II?" In a funny sort of way, the entire Abbey community was on edge, waiting for an update about news from the war.

And I would tell them.

I told them about how difficult the officer training was at Tower Hall in Chicago. Training was intense—detailed mathematical, navigational, mechanical, and tactical lessons. Examinations were difficult. Poor exam results were "treed," that is to say, displayed publically. "Treeing" signified that a candidate's officer status was in peril and that the route was about to get much more difficult. Nothing had prepared these young men for the

Dogmatic Slumber

true gravity of war. They were preparing in a classroom to do something, something they had never done before, something or a series of somethings bearing life or death consequences. The tone of my father's letters from Tower Hall was anxious, uncertain, ominous, and foreboding. He wondered where he was going and what he would face when he got there. Europe? Japan? Africa? Chicago was farther away than he'd ever been from home.

I told them about the rough and stormy passage across the Atlantic. My father's LCT craft was portaged by a larger, cargo-laden LST. The LST was battered all the way as it crossed the Atlantic, listing heavily with 30-degree rolls alternating from port to starboard incessantly in five-second intervals. It was a terrible voyage that sickened most of the young crew. My father wrote that he held his own.

I told them about the confusion that reigned during the early training exercises in the theater of war. Training orders were not well-coordinated. Communication was sketchy. "What are our orders? What are the coordinates? Not sure. I follow you or you follow me? The hell with it—here we go! I think we're heading the wrong way! Where are we supposed to be?!!! When? What are we supposed to do now? Christ! Eight-foot swells! How do you steer through this shit?!!! I suppose as best you can. Never beached before! Is this the spot? Who knows?!!! Christ, here goes! Wham! Did we break the prop? Does anyone know how to fix a broken prop? I think we're OK. Let's get the hell out of here!"

I told them about how woefully unprepared the crew was for the treacherous road that lay ahead. My father's battle testing was exclusively in the class room, not at the helm of this 114-foot-long landing craft. And yet, his training was far superior to that of the eleven-man crew. They had almost none. The crew's assignments were awarded almost randomly without regard to training or talent. The cook did not know how. He became known as "Spam" Speyers, a moniker he earned due to his one-dimensional culinary repertoire—spam any way you like it!

I told them about the first air raid at port in Italy, the first of over 300. It was a dark, calm night when the shrill sirens sounded, urgent and alarming. This was real and coming quickly upon them. The first wave of German planes emerged from the dark. Flying low over the harbor, the first planes dropped flash sticks to illuminate the targets, stationary ships at port. The second wave came with bombs. Chaos! There was a series of blinding and deafening explosions. Several ships across the way were hit and ablaze. The harbor was shrouded in thick, black, acrimonious layers of smoke. Just off the stern of my father's ship, a thunderous detonation exploded. A wall of seawater crashed onto the deck. Shrapnel pierced the ship's shell, clanging and ringing—metal on metal. "Get down! Duck! Cover! Run! Nowhere to run to!" The scene was frightening calamity. Unbelievably loud and dangerous noise, insidious smoke, and hellish fire filled the air. Allied searchlights frantically sought out a German target, finally latching onto a single German plane. Guns trained on the target. *Boom! Boom! Boom!* The plane was hit. It ignited, smoke and fire streamed from its tail. The plane shuttered and stalled before cartwheeling and smashing into the water then plunging to the sea right out there—right there—a few hundred feet away. The nameless German boy flying that plane was now dead.

And just like that, the raid was over. Death was in the harbor. Damage was yet to be assessed. But the only assessment that really mattered was one: Were you alive or not? What a horrific thing that first air raid was, a horrific thing that would be repeated over and over again during the course of the war. This was the first of hundreds of air raids that my father would endure. He would survive, but he would also carry the trauma with him throughout the rest of his life, trying to forget but unable.

I told them about the day my father loaned his second in command to pilot another LCT. The other ship's captain had an errand to run that day and needed a substitute. My father's ship was trailing shortly behind the other when the torpedo stuck, an explosion that delivered a lethal wallop. The blast came from nowhere and sent shrapnel to the heavens, along with every soldier onboard the other ship. My father carried out the grim task of collecting the bodies, including his second, and then towing the skeletal remains of the destroyed vessel back to port. Later that day he wrote a letter to his crewman's widow. And as he wrote, he began to change forever. His mood darkened. Soon he would begin to lean on alcohol. And from that point on, depression and alcohol would guide the trajectory of his life. He would return home much different than the young man who left to go to war.

I told them about the unbearable heat of the African siroccos, like a blast furnace, the stinging wind-driven sands that blew in from the desert, the flies, the fleas, the other pests, and the scorching, inescapable sun. The heat was unbearable. There was no relief.

I told them about the unending hours of sheer boredom and the intense longing for home, for the things he loved, about the timeless and aching lulls between the last and the next horrifying eruption of war. My father did not write about courage or patriotism. He wrote about the senselessness of the war and reproached the world leaders who declared it. No one knew about the Nazi death camps. The "righteousness" of the war didn't come into focus until it was over. My father didn't want to be there. He didn't want to kill anyone; he certainly didn't want to be killed; and he couldn't live with the thought of someone else dying in his place. He also felt a tremendous responsibility, an almost unbearable burden, to protect his crew. He wrote about the weight, about how the decisions he made and his skill in piloting the ship were the difference between life and death for the young men in his crew. This burden wore on him. There were many letters where he seemed to give up hope that the war would ever end, that he would live to come out the other side of these gates of hell. Sometimes he would write, telling my mother about his dreams for the life they would live and the family they would raise together. Other times he would write that he probably wasn't going to make it. She should prepare to go on without him.

I told them about how the growing depression in my father's spirit became increasingly visible over time. It was all taking a toll on him. His nerves were "shot." He described how loud noises now made him jump and threw him into an inescapable state of panic and alarm. He had Post Traumatic Syndrome without diagnosis and without treatment other than his self-prescription of alcohol. I could mark the stages of my father's depression as I read letter after letter. And for the first time, I understood.

I told them about the day the ship was at rest in a quiet bay in Italy. On shore a German tank emerged from the trees and began shelling the craft. This was a dangerous scenario. *Boom! Boom! Boom!* The ship was defenseless, a sitting duck. Suddenly, like the cavalry to the rescue, a gargantuan British warship swept into the bay, nearly swamping my father's much smaller craft. The giant battleship quickly trained its massive guns on the enemy tank and began blasting away. My father wrote, "That was the last we heard from that tank."

I told them about some of the lighter moments, which were few. The crew adopted a small, sweet, black and white puppy from North Africa. The crew fell in love with her and named her "Gertie" from Bizerte. A dog on board was, of course, against naval regulations. So the crew devised ways to hide Gertie when the commander came along to perform inspections. This little puppy was one of the only aspects of the crew's life at war that resembled the normalcy of life back home.

These men loved that dog. My father never said and I am left to wonder what became of her.

I told them about the day when four Italian soldiers walked out onto the pier where the LCT was docked. They came to surrender. The Italians were friendly and helpful. They made friends with their "captors" and swabbed the decks to earn their keep. My father gave them each a U.S. Naval cap, which they wore proudly, even on the day the MPs came to take them into formal custody. All four smiled and waved their caps to the ship's crew as the MPs took them away, their jeep climbing the dusty hill heading away from the port.

I told them about the games of bridge my father would organize to help pass the time, about the small library he built and traded when he could, about the play he wrote and entitled *The Dark Ages.* The play was an engaging science fiction story about the near end of the earth. There were just a few individuals left to carry on, isolated in a faraway place. They had the ability travel around the world and to choose which individuals should be brought back to life. Those chosen would join the few survivors left to restart civilization. The story evolved into an interesting moral dilemma. Given the chance to restart society, what elements of humanity should be retained and what elements left behind? My father was trying to understand the forces that had created the war and what a warless utopian society might look like.

I told them about stories and I showed them pictures: a picture of the cute little dog, Gertie; a picture of my father in dress whites standing strongly next to my mother before going off to war, he handsome, she beautiful, both smiling; a picture of the crew, butt naked, running to jump off the deck and into the water; another picture of the crew huddled beneath a pilfered army tent, the only means to escape the punishing African sun; a picture presumed to be of Cecil Pointer, the second in command, smiling, behind him a wall pocked with shrapnel, all before he was killed by torpedo attack; and a picture of my father on the deck of LCT 290, dressed in a t-shirt and kakis, hands on hips, smiling weakly but unable to hide the despair lurking in his eyes

I told them about and read some of the well-worded, clever, and passionate passages from these letters, many referencing poetry favored by my father. My father had a love for poetry and in incomprehensible ability to recite lengthy passages from memory.

I told them about *My Travels* by Ima Sea-Chest, another creative endeavor born from his efforts to pass time. My father described his journey, the ports of call, and the horrors of war all through the inanimate eyes of his companion sea chest. I read aloud some of the more interesting entries.

January 1943. Born in the basement of 1338 46th St., Des Moines, Iowa.

January 25. Left by express for New York.

April 4. A memorable day. To pier #51, New York Harbor, and aboard U.S.S., LST 352

> **April 6.** In the Gulf Stream, and was it ever rough!
>
> **May 4.** Oran, North Africa, and transferred to U.S.S. LCT 290
>
> **July 7.** Thirty-odd days of boredom, and 30 nights of air raids; under way to Sicily.
>
> **September 7.** Salerno, Italy. "D" day, "H" hour plus 20 minutes
>
> **February 9.** Anzio Harbor (as of today, Hell Harbor). Who's kidding whom?
>
> **May 4.** Palermo Harbor. The war seems far away. But where are we going?
>
> **June 3.** Where did everyone go?
>
> **June 6.** To Normandy!
>
> **September 21.** Here we go home!
>
> **October 2, 1944.** Boston, Mass., U.S.A!
>
> **November 22, 1945.** Home again!
>
> **August 10, 1967.** Hey, I'm out of retirement! Hear they're repainting me and shipping me off to a women's dorm at Columbia, Univ. What a fate for an old Navy chest!

I told them about an impromptu chain letter from home written one evening around the family dinner table. Each person—my father's parents, his brothers and sister, and my mother—each wrote a few lines. They wrote about relatively mundane events, inquired as to his safety, and wished for his quick return. My mother had made the meal. The potatoes didn't come out right. My uncle JB, a little boy at the time, wrote that he didn't understand the ruckus about the potatoes. He thought they were fine. I'm sure that my father cherished mundane comments like this from family at home. At least for a few moments, he was granted solace. If he closed his eyes and concentrated, he could pretend he was there with them. At least in the recesses of his mind, he could recall the world back home that he loved, not the one that he was in.

I told them about the tardy flow and limited availability of information. The young soldiers were so far away from home, most for the first time. They hungered for any thread of information about what was going on in the outside world, what was happening back home, and how the war was going. The updates, however, were scarce and erratic. The long interludes between letters from home were insufferable. My father's depression sank deeper when a single day would grow into several days, or sometimes weeks, without a letter from my mother. She was writing each and every day, but delivery was not keeping pace. My father's spirits soared when the drought was finally broken, sometimes by a bundle of five or maybe six letters arriving together simultaneously.

I told them about how it was the same for my mother. She hungered for news. Was her husband alright? Was he alive?!!! Mail delivery from the war, whether it came by V-Mail or on standard U.S. Naval letterhead, was also unpredictable. Her letters documented her agony as she waited for the mail and there would be none. The worst moment undoubtedly came as D-Day unfolded. All that my mother could know was what was reported in the news. A massive invasion was underway, with many casualties accruing to the Allied troops. She knew that Wayne must be part of it. She did not know if he was alive or dead. And she did not know that all military correspondence flowing from the European theater had been suspended as of May 23. The Allied Forces wanted to ensure against any unintentional leaks about the invasion. All she knew was that her husband was most likely in the middle of it and several weeks had passed without word from him. The pain, the panic, the worry were unabated and all-consuming.

I told them about my father's last letter. He was coming home! He wrote that he would be back "around Dick's birthday, not to the port I left from, but the one to the north." This message was code, intended to provide details that otherwise would not survive the censor's scissors. Translated, Wayne was returning on or about his younger brother Dick's birthday (October 1) and to the port north of his departure port, which had been New York (thus Boston). The letter closed with this:

> "That is about as definite as I can write now, and it's all the more that you'll hear from me from this side of the ocean—or any other ocean ever, I hope! It's with the greatest of pleasure that I resign my position as your favorite correspondent. It would suit me perfectly to

> never write another letter to you, i.e. never necessary to write—speech is so much nicer and easier.
>
> So, while you're waiting for my phone call, you can close "book one of my husband's letters to me," tie a pretty pink ribbon around the bundle, toss 'em in a corner to be discovered by your grandchildren sometime 60 or 70 years from now. Bet they'll think you were quite a gal! And I'll further bet quotations from some would make the sweet old girl blush a bit too.
>
> I wonder if you'll remember my voice? It will be nice to hear yours again. And until I do.
>
> All my love, Wayne"

I told them about my father walking into the officer's club once he arrived in Boston. From behind, someone firmly gripped his shoulder. "How are you, Wayne?" It was his brother, Frank! This was such an amazing chance reunion for two brothers in the war, one returning from the Mediterranean and the other just heading off to the Pacific. The raw emotions of that surprise encounter were surely overpowering. Family lore has it that Frank posed as Wayne the next day and went to pick up his leave assignment. That gave my father a jump on catching the first train to the north shore of Chicago to meet up with Edith.

I told them about Wayne's phone call to Edith from Boston, the first time they had heard each other's voices in more than eighteen months. Edith was employed in the bookkeeping department of a Des Moines insurance company. Her supervisor came out to tell her that

Wayne was on the phone. She brought her hands to her face, clutched her heart and gasped, then leapt from her desk to rush to the phone. The entire department scuttled away, vacated the area, and left her to share with Wayne and Wayne alone what must have been the most glorious and emotion-filled moment of her life.

And as I finished reading the last letter, I paused. I was by myself, alone in the middle of France. I had many strong emotions as I read along. Those emotions came back to me all at once, like a deluge. There were times when I had laughed. At other times I was simply amazed. But most often I was choked with tears, with rising swells of something, something very powerful that I could not name—not sadness, but yes sadness; not regret, but yes regret; not pride, but yes pride. Almost against my will, something important was happening between my father and me. I was coming to understand him in a way that I never had before.

For the first time in my life, I truly began to think about forgiveness, how difficult and essential it was. Love, respect, and admiration were emerging from my heart.

Chapter 11
Paris

Paris was a short two-hour train ride from several towns close to Pontlevoy. Trains to Paris ran from Montrichard, Onzain, Blois, and Tours regularly. I took advantage of the easy access and travelled to Paris twice, once early on for a long weekend and later on for nearly a week.

The weekend trip was a jaunt with a large handful of students chaperoned by Keenon, Ben, Catherine, Doug, and me. Doug was planning to fly back to the states at the end of the weekend, so this was the last shot for him and me to have a whirl until his return in April. And we did, in fact, live large that weekend in Paris.

I had been to Paris a handful of times and had a reasonably well-defined sense for the city's attraction and layout. However, seeing Paris with the likes of Doug and Catherine, who lived in Paris for several years, opened up new frontiers, off-the-beaten-path neighborhoods, and lesser traveled arrondissements. We stayed at a two-star hotel tucked away in the 19th arrondissement near Le Baissin de la Villette, a long manmade rectangle of water which connected the Canal de l'Ourcq to the Canal St-Martin. A tree-lined park ran the full the length of the Villette. Beyond the park the neighborhood was lively and bustling.

Few tourists make it to the 19th. There were no famous landmarks or tourist sites, but the neighborhood was quintessential. In the morning, crews of strong young men rowed back and forth along the length of the Villette. On weekdays young businessmen with slick-backed hair and thin, fitted suits walked briskly to work holding cell phones to their ears. In the afternoon, old men rolled bocce balls in the park, young mothers pushed their babies around in strollers, and lovers strolled hand in hand. The surrounding streets were busy. Sidewalk cafes lined the streets. Thin, smart-looking young women with short haircuts sat outside in cafe chairs reading newspapers or chatting while they smoked unfiltered cigarettes and sipped sugared café noirs with cream. At night ethnic restaurants—African Couscous, East Indian, Vietnamese, Chinese, Middle Eastern—came alive and all blended together to create a wonderful potpourri of flavors and smells. Watching life play out in the 19th was to witness Paris as it truly is, one of the world's great cities.

On the first day, Doug and I struck off from the hotel with a small pack of six to eight students. We walked from the hotel through the back streets of Paris towards the Louvre, probably a couple of miles. We paused frequently to taste Paris—gelato, roasted chestnuts, hotdogs tucked into small, fresh baguettes, and warm crêpes filled with spinach and brie. I bought a Parisienne sandwich—a thin slice of ham, emmental cheese, and butter on a long, thin baguette, crispy outside, moist and chewy inside—so simple. Of all the material things in the world, a Parisienne sandwich is the best thing I have known. If I had a choice in the matter, it would be my last meal.

As we walked, Doug explained the architecture as we transitioned from one ethnic neighborhood to the next. We stopped in front of an elementary school where a bouquet of flowers was placed on the wall by a plaque. Doug explained the meaning; prior to the onset of World War II the French worked hand in hand with the Nazis to round up Jewish children from the schools and deport them. The bouquets were placed there by the government and freshened daily as a quiet acknowledgement and reminder of what happened.

Walking through Paris streets filled the students with joyous wonder. When we reached the Louvre, Doug and I separated from the students and left them to explore and to find their own ways. At first they were intimidated by the prospect. They not only survived, but thrived. That night they all captured pictures of their friends standing before the Eifel Tower, the tower illuminated with glowing white lights, the students with beaming smiles. They were falling in love with Paris.

Doug and I met up with Catherine and the three of us spent the late afternoon and evening walking from one of Catherine's favorite places to the next.

Everywhere we went was different and wonderful. The taste, the vibrancy, the culture, the spirit of Paris brought our senses to life. We sampled hors d'oeuvres—Mediterranean olives mixed with tangy preserved lemons, mysterious terrines seasoned with garlic and pepper, and sharp fresh cheeses. We drank glass after glass of bold red wine—St. Emelion, Bordeaux, Haut Medoc, and Chateauneuf du Pape. We talked and laughed deep into the night before finally boarding the Metro back to the hotel.

The next morning, Doug had some business to attend to and I set off on my own walking along the Canal St-Martin down to the Bastille. At times the canal flowed above ground and at times below. I walked along the canal, crossing over bridges and watching as small boats sparsely filled with tourists made their way through the locks. I waded through the wonderful scents emanating from diverse ethnic food spots: curries, roasting chickens, blends of Far East heat, and freshly baking bread. The entire length of the canal was lined with trees and park-like settings and blotched with restaurants, small sidewalk cafes, and boulangeries. I ducked into a small boulangerie, indistinguishable from the others, and met paradise in the form of an almond croissant. The pastry was ethereal, filled with delicious sweetness, dusted with powdered sugar, and sprinkled with toasted almonds. It was Nirvana—flakey, buttery, and filled with indescribable, sweet, chewy goodness. I had another, and then wished for tomorrow when I could have another.

I continued on and eventually arrived at the Bastille Market, a lively Sunday morning festival with musicians, food vendors, antique dealers, clothiers, and ethnic craftsmen. The market was overflowing with colors, activity, and flavor. I ordered a crêpe and watched as the crêpièr smoothed the batter on the hot surface of the skillet, filled the bubbling crêpe with sausage, basil, onions, and cheese, and folded it into a triangular pocket. The deliciousness sustained me as I walked among the throng of vendors and shoppers.

Later that afternoon I met up with Doug in the Jewish Marais. Doug described our meeting place: "The Place de Voges. There's a statue of Louis XIII riding a horse. I'll meet you underneath the horse's ass!" This was an easy enough landmark to find and sufficiently specific. We found each other there and breezed around the Marais, perhaps Paris's most endearing neighborhood. The Marais is full of odd curiosity shops, neatly stacked homes, and small restaurants. And once again, the smell of food permeated the streets. This time it was the falafel sandwiches—fresh and chewy pitas stuffed with garlicky chickpeas, hummus, pickled red cabbage, and salted cucumbers.

We browsed the Marais, walked past a home where Victor Hugo once lived, then wandered across the Seine to the Latin Quarter and past places that had once been home to Descartes and Hemmingway. We walked through La Sorbonne and up the hill, where we stumbled across the Arenes de Lutèce, an ancient Roman amphitheater nested in the middle of Paris. Inside the arena, young school girls sat on the stone seats and chatted in the sun while young boys ran about kicking soccer balls on the sand where gladiators once fought.

As the afternoon lengthened and night began to fall, we took the Metro back across the river to Montparnasse. The world's best crêpes are made there. I ordered one with chevre, spinach, walnuts, and an oozing baked egg—ooh la la! Doug and I split a carafe of crisp, dry white wine to go with our crêpes before finding the closest Metro stop to catch a train home.

What a day to remember, just like every day in Paris. At the end of it, I took a moment to reflect. Paris was such a sensual place, a great place to be aware of your senses and your thoughts, a great place to be in the moment, a great place to notice and appreciate what's happening—now—the intense taste and texture of that almond croissant, the smiling face of the little French girl riding the merry-go-round, the bright colors of the fruit stands at the market, the beauty of this painting or that sculpture, the fascination of our conversation. Paris was not a place to dwell on problems that had already happened, to be nervous about what might go wrong in the future, to wait for something better to happen at some point later on. Paris was a place to take notice that you were alive and to be in love with the notion that you were. Why shouldn't I carry that notion with me every day no matter where I was? I vowed to try.

The following morning, Doug took an early flight back to the States. The rest of us boarded the train for Blois and returned to Pontlevoy. The students couldn't stop talking about what had just happened to them. A few short days ago they had arrived in a small French village, intimidated by the prospect of simply ordering a croissant at the local bakery. They now knew how to navigate all of Paris, see the sights, shop for clothes, go to museums, ride the Metro, take a cab, walk without getting lost, and order plates of some of the most wonderful food on the planet. For me, to have seen Paris was great. To have seen it through the wide and excited eyes of these young students was all the better.

Several weeks later we returned to Paris, this time with all of the students and faculty. Doug's brilliant design of the Abbey program included a three-part journey out and away from Pontlevoy:

The first part was "Paris Week," when the classroom moved to Paris so that the students could immerse themselves in the city's history, art, and culture. Paris week was followed by a trip to Bayeux, a day at the Normandy beaches, and a few days in Amsterdam.

The second part was called "AbbeyROAD," where the students separated into three factions of their choice. One group flew to Dublin to study Irish literature; one group flew to Rome to study art; and the third group took the train to Berlin to learn more about WWII.

The third part was each student's individual "Vision Quest." The concept here was for each student to go off on their own, to pick a path, a place, an experience that was uniquely their own. The assignment included the responsibility to return with a story. What happened? Why did they choose that experience as their Vision

Quest? What impact did the experience have on them? What did they learn? Why was it important?

This alluring three-part interlude began with the better part of a week spent in Paris. The students stayed in a hostel. The faculty and I stayed the same 19th district hotel, where Doug, I, and the others had stayed previously.

During the course of our week in Paris, I frequently met up with students and staff—sometimes for breakfast, sometimes for dinner, sometimes for a walkabout, once for aperitifs at Elizabeth's rental flat in the Marais, once at Catherine's favorite Vietnamese restaurant, Dong Huong, once for coffee and thick, decadent hot chocolate at Deux Magots and so on.

But by and large I was on my own. I walked and walked and walked. I must have walked more than ten miles a day—along the Seine, beside the canals, back through the Marais, Montparnasse, and Montmartre. I walked without a specific purpose or destination. My only plan was not to have one. I lost myself in Paris. Uncertain what lay around the corner, I simply walked. By and large, I went unnoticed by others. I was invisible. I watched, observed, and took in the colors, the sounds, and the smells—more almond croissants, more Bordeaux wines, sewer and street urine smells mingling with funky East Indian curries, street musicians, mimes, ice skating rinks, merry-go-rounds, and market places filled with colorful vendors purveying fresh fruits and vegetables, sausages and cheeses, freshly plucked chickens and ducks, skinned rabbits, olive carts, fresh fish, mussels, and oysters.

It snowed one day, which was at the same time both magical and miserable. The falling snow was extraordinary as Paris became blanketed in a beautiful new light. The beauty, however, was delusional and only skin deep. It was also wickedly cold. The wind-whipped snow stung my face as I walked. The sidewalks were precarious and mostly unshoveled. I was reminded of my invisibility when I slipped and fell on a crowded sidewalk. No one took notice, which made me glad and angry at the same time. I dusted myself off and kept on walking, head down.

Needing to get out of the weather, I ended up at the Musée d'Orsay. I had been to d'Orsay before and was well aware of its superb impressionist art collection and its fantastic interior space—a renovated, art deco train station from a bygone era. What attracted me on this day, however, was a special exhibit: L'Ange du Bizarre, or Angels of the Strange. This exhibit was wonderfully disturbing, constructed around dark romanticism and the emergence of menacing and ominous forces in art—dark images, deformities, demons, empty and threatening landscapes, sometimes realistic, sometimes surreal, foreboding images of mental anguish, despair, and fear.

As I moved from room to room throughout the exhibit, I saw sculptures, photographs, paintings, and old black and white movie clips playing, clips from films such as from *Nosferatu*—all of it creepy, unsavory, disturbing, murky, and moody. The images were unwanted and yet irresistible, images that bubbled up from somewhere deep down in the artist's psyche. The exhibit shaped an uncomfortable awareness of one's own dark, unwanted thoughts, thoughts that lurk somewhere beneath the surface, thoughts which are better left unexplored and unnourished, but which are nonetheless always present, always part of who we are. These dark thoughts occasionally rise up from the subconscious to the surface of our awareness despite our best efforts to ignore and suppress them.

The next day I went to the Louvre, a no less interesting, but certainly more uplifting, experience. Terry suggested I go there with the promise that I spend no more than two hours there. "Any more is too much," he warned me.

I had been to the Louvre twice in my life and must honestly confess that I found those experiences overwhelming and unpleasurable. Several years ago, Laura and I did attend a small exhibit at the Louvre made up of several Michelangelo sketchings. That experience was exquisite, in part because we were able to view that exhibit without entering the immensity of Louvre proper. In any event, for the better part of 40 years, I have considered the Louvre to be too big, too difficult to navigate, and too overrun with tourists.

All that changed for me using Terry's advice, "Two hours and no more." With that strategy as my guide, my afternoon at the Louvre this time was remarkable. I saw "Hermaphrodite Sleeping," an unbelievable creation, life emerging from alabaster stone; her beauty astounding, the artistic achievement incredible. The same can be said for "Venus de Milo," the embodiment of perfection. I slowly circled her, closely, marveling and contemplating the impossibility that she was created from stone by the hand of man.

The Renaissance paintings were beyond extraordinary. Leonardo da Vinci's "John the Baptist" in particular arrested me with its perfect sfumato strokes, the smile akin to Mona Lisa's, the finger playfully and uncertainly pointing delicately to heaven, the element of doubt revealed in the gesture, and the hint of self-portraiture. Veronese's "Wedding Feast of Cana" hung massively on the wall opposite "Mona Lisa." This painting astonished me. More than 30 feet wide, a human landscape too huge, too colorful, too vibrant, too detailed, too wonderful, and too monumental to believe. The painting was every bit the miracle as was Jesus's first, that of turning water to wine, which was said to have occurred at this feast. Gericault's "Raft of Medusa" clawed at me, forcing me to stop and ponder as I walked by. The painting, of starving men adrift in a literal sea of despair, brought to life all of the sensations of misery that had been conjured the day before at L'Ange du Bizarre at D'Orsay.

And just like that, my two hours at the Louvre were up. Had I stayed longer, the power of the experience doubtlessly would have been eroded by overstimulation. As it was, my visit to the Louvre was the most powerful of experiences, a transcendental exposure to art at its highest level.

What a contrast it was between my bookend experiences at the Louvre and the Musée D'Orsay. One museum platform revealed the dark side of the human spirit. The other displayed the soaring heights that artistic expression can reach when divinely inspired. Taking Terry's art class had heightened my interest in the creative process. Juxtaposed against each other, I saw firsthand how the tension between the horrific and the sublime has stoked art's creation throughout the ages.

Dogmatic Slumber

Crêpièr—Bastille Market

Market fruits and vegetables

Fruits de mer

Merry-go-round near the Marais

Dogmatic Slumber

Canal Quai Valmy—Paris

Arenes de Lutèce Roman Amphitheater

Ice skating at the Hotel des Invalides

With Kevin at Les Deux Magots

Dogmatic Slumber

Statue near the Louvre

Cain

Poster for L'Ange du Bizzarre

Raft of Medusa

Hermaphrodite Sleeping

Wedding Feast of Cana (width 32 ½ feet)

Venus de Milo

John the Baptist

Chapter 12
It Happened on a
Bus Ride to Bayeux

At the end of our week in Paris, we boarded a bus for Bayeux, a nice medium-sized town situated in northern France near the English Channel. There was a spectacular gothic cathedral in Bayeux, but the town was best known for the Bayeux Tapestry, an immense, embroidered cloth, 230 feet long and nearly 1,000 years old. The tapestry pictorially re-told the story of the Norman invasion of England. The battle was historically important and the tapestry's sheer size and provenance amazing, but truth be told, I found the artistic renderings childlike and uninspiring. There, someone had to say it.

What I did find inspiring was the bus ride to Bayeux. Sitting on that bus I experienced a moment like no others in my life, a defining moment that I will always remember, a moment that changed me forever. In retrospect, I would come to understand that perhaps my entire life had been a journey to arrive at this moment.

I was sitting by myself, gazing absently through the window as a rather unremarkable countryside passed by on the other side of the glass. I had just finished reading my parents' letters and was working up both my thoughts and my courage. I had promised the students that I would share my parents' story the following day at Normandy. I was struggling.

Ben was seated behind me lecturing a student about the finer points of Muslim religious history. I could overhear the conversation, but wasn't attentive. I drifted off into an inner world of my own. My consciousness granulated, uncomfortably. I felt a tightening in my chest. I was keenly aware of the need to breathe and had to concentrate to do so. A heaving wave of emotion stirred deep within, nearly suffocating me.

I concentrated and reflected upon my parents' story, the story as it had been revealed to me in their correspondences. The sum of the words simply overcame me, the agony of their separation, the fear, the unbearable possibility that they might never see each other again, the future lives they so desperately dreamed of sharing, the longing, the pain, the loneliness, the endless hours, days, weeks, and months of waiting, the impossibly slow passage of time, and the constant, dull ache of missing each other.

From my father's perspective, I thought about the war's lethal calamity, its horrifying rage, outrageous and deafening sounds, blinding explosive flashes, and the charred, acrid smell of human death. I thought about the two things my parents shared: love for each other and a desperate recurring question that seemed to have no answer. Would they ever be together again?

I felt their emotions as if they were my own. I choked and sputtered, closing my eyes to block out the rest of the world. I felt extremely vulnerable, riddled with a sense of guilt and shame. I felt guilt for so readily and harshly judging my father all these years, for not making a better effort to understand him. I felt shame for never having given him his due for what he went through during the war, for not being sympathetic towards him for the suffering he endured at the unrelenting hands of the demons that followed him back home.

Sharing these newfound, raw emotions would be very difficult. Could I possibly do it without breaking down? I bounced back and forth. Bail out or tell the story? Was there a way to tell the story without going too deep, without getting too personal? Could I keep my composure and get through it once I started? Truthfully, if someone had interrupted me at that very moment, while these thoughts were tossing in my head, and asked me to speak, I could not have done so without weeping. I was really struggling here, alone, by myself, in my own world.

I braced myself, took a deep breath, and exhaled. I resolved myself to it. I'd find a way. I had to. It was important for others to hear the story. More importantly, I needed to tell it.

As I churned these thoughts in my head, I also began to reflect on my own life. I realized that I was somehow changing in an important way. I was softening. I was forgiving. I was awakening. Barriers were falling. Closed doors were opening. I was becoming more alert to different possibilities and perspectives. I sifted through the lifelong collage of experiences which summed to me. I slowed when I came to the most recent happenings since leaving home. I paused when I thought about meeting Terry Netter. And with that pause, there and then, I made an unexpected and dramatic choice that I never could have planned or imagined.

I chose to believe in God.

At that moment, things changed for me, irreversibly, forever. There I sat, alone on the bus. I smiled gently. I was at peace. I was calm. I felt as though I had been carrying around a heavy bag full of things my entire life, things that had no use, things that were holding me back, things that were closing me off to joy, things like competiveness, like resentment, like dogmatic certainty. I didn't even realize that I was carrying that bag, but once I dropped it, I immediately knew that from that point on I could travel more freely and experience things with a more open, joyous heart. Right there, right then, that's the way it came to me.

There must be a God—not a Christian God or a Buddhist God or a Hindu God or anyone else's God. As far as I was concerned, there are aspects of truth in each theology, but aspects of each that don't ring properly for me as well. I accept God's existence, but I am not well able to articulate what that means. I cannot describe or define God. God, to me, remains mysterious and unintelligible to the human mind, too complicated to understand. God is something to be wondered at, always over the horizon, beyond reach, incomprehensible, untouchable, and infinite. God is beyond our reckoning.

Sitting alone on that bus somewhere between Paris and Bayeux in northern France, that was the moment and the place where I awoke from my dogmatic slumber. Dogma can be such an unproductive thing. It can cause us to close doors to different perspectives simply because those perspectives may weaken or challenge the beliefs we hold. We might tend to surround ourselves only with people who think like we do. We might tend to shout loudly so that we don't have to hear what the other person has to say. That's true for dogmatic believers as well as for non-believers. In its strongest form, dogma causes us to ridicule, hate, or destroy those who think differently than we do. History is full of intolerant and violent acts carried out in the name of God. Consider the Holy Wars, the Crusades, the Holocaust, the Middle East, or the modern day conflict between extreme Christians and extreme Muslims.

For me, my personal dogma had denied my considering a different perspective, a different way to assess the possibility of God's existence. I had been certain. But I was wrong.

Prior to this moment, I had reasoned the concept of God using only the path of logic. Science and observable phenomena had been my shepherds. They told me that God did not exist. I now realized that science could take us a long way, perhaps someday to both the beginning and the end of the universe. But science cannot explain feelings, or imagination, or creativity. Science cannot account for the human soul. Science can neither observe nor understand God.

The change for me was meeting Terry Netter. Terry didn't intend to, but he showed me how to follow a different path to God. I learned to look inward, not outward. I chose the moral, intuitive path rather than the logical, empirical path to comprehend God. The path Terry showed me lacked a single thread of evidence, had no proof, and did not involve a shard of logic. This path came from the gut and was based upon instinctive reason. My mind had intuitively and instinctively come in tune with the truth of things, the truth that there was a God.

Some may agree and some may disagree with that postulate, and that it up to them. I am certainly not on a mission to convince others. But for me God has to exist. If not from God, from where else does the human spirit come? What else could be the inspiration for the world's great art, music, poetry, and dance? How else can we explain love? There must be a creating force. There must be a purpose. There must be a connection that we share with others, with those that went before us, with those that share our moments, and with those that will follow.

There is a choice that we make of our own free will to be good and kind, or not. Every day we are confronted with news about people who make the wrong choice, who commit acts of hate, violence, and selfishness. There is suffering all over the world. Suffering is not God's will. It is not God's fault. It is ours. God has planted a spirit within us to guide us. Sometimes we lose our way. But the human spirit is at its best, is closest to its purpose, and is nearest fulfillment and how it is intended to be when it soars through expressions of love, kindness, and beauty. These things come from God. These things are in our nature. These things bring us in harmony with each other and with God. This harmony is God

I will no doubt always have doubt, for there is no way to know for certain. I realize that, in a sense, all that I have really done is to put forth a hypothesis that God exists. I have confidence in this hypothesis, but I cannot prove it. I have confidence that my instinctive reason has allowed me to guess accurately about the existence and the nature of a divine power, a guess that is no better than anyone else's, but a guess that is best for me. My guess is that something created my soul and organized a place and a purpose for it to exist. Whatever happens at the end of life, my energy, my spirit, my soul—whatever I should call it—will not dissipate. It is part of something big building to something bigger yet. And I will in some way, in some form, be part of it. That's my guess. It's more than a guess. It's what I believe to be true. To me that notion is comforting, and powerful.

I realize that my faith is juvenile and still developing. It may always be that way. I need to learn more, and I am open to learning as much as I possibly can. For instance, I am not a Christian. But people are still talking today about Jesus Christ more than 2,000 years after his death. He must have had something interesting to say. I'd like to know more about what it was. I'm also eager to consider other spiritual disciplines. None of them can be entirely right, and yet most of them must contain some elements of truth.

As I sat on that bus to Bayeux, I kept all of this to myself. I alone was aware of this inner dialogue. I thought about how the belief in God's existence might affect me. I determined that it should bring a more personal focus on people, kindness, compassion, and joy. This marked a huge transformation from the man who had been rushing through life, earning wages, collecting things, and, in many ways, connecting with people more or less sporadically as time permitted. I boarded the bus in Paris as that man. I got off the bus in Bayeux a different man.

Chapter 13
Normandy

We spent the night in Bayeux. The next morning we boarded a bus headed to the Normandy beaches. We planned to visit Arromanches, Omaha Beach, Pointe-du-Hoc, and both the German and American cemeteries. I was committed and prepared to share Wayne and Edith's story with the group when we came to the American cemetery. My inner dialogue had fortified me, and I was looking forward to the opportunity. I was still filled with pangs of emotion. But I had gained confidence that I could hold it together. On the heels of a day to remember, this was going to be another, my own personal day of days.

Our first stop was Arromanches, where the Allied Forces assembled the artificial Mulberry Harbor during the invasion's earliest days. As I looked out upon the sunken remains of the once-floating harbor, I was reminded of the invasion's logistical complexities. Gaining a toehold on the beachheads was one thing.

Providing for the 1,000,000 troops within days of their landing was an enormous undertaking as well. Food, ammunition, electronics, tanks, jeeps, fuel, medical supplies, and so on all had to be delivered and coordinated.

I noticed a small plaque positioned down by the sea wall at Arromanches that garnered my attention and probably no one else's. The plaque was put in place by the British Landing Ship Tank (LST) and Landing Craft Tank (LCT) Association in honor of the British sailors and royal marines who lost their lives securing the Normandy beaches. This plaque had special meaning to me. My father was the sole American member of the British Landing Craft Association. During the war, my father made lifelong friends with several of his British LCT peers. And for many years he and my mother traveled to London each November to attend the British LCT reunions. My father was inaugurated as the only United States member of the British LCT Association and also served one year as the Association's president. I stood over the plaque for quite some time, pointed it out to a few students, and smiled as I captured a picture to share with my sisters.

Our next stop was Omaha Beach, a beautiful beach in much the same way most beaches are beautiful—steep, verdant hills falling away to fine white sand and clear blue water. But Omaha will always be haunted by the scores of souls that perished during those early days of June, 1944. As I walked the beach, it was a very pleasant day. But I could not shake the awareness that I was walking in footsteps that had been washed away so many years ago, footsteps owned by thousands of courageous young men. In a very real sense, those footsteps will remain on the beach sands of Normandy forever. As I walked, I was filled with an immense sense of awe and pride. These men had been called. And I couldn't help but wonder how I would have responded had the same been true for me. I knew how my father responded. I hoped that I would have been as strong.

Our next stop, Pointe-du-Hoc, was a much different place than Omaha. Strategically important, Pointe-du-Hoc was a steep, craggy cliff overlooking the English Channel, the highest lookout point between Utah Beach to the West and Omaha Beach to the East. The Germans had fortified Pointe-du-Hoc with concrete casings and gun pits. During the planning of the invasion, the Allied forces determined that taking out Pointe-du-Hoc prior to the landing was critical to the invasion's success. It wasn't going to be easy, and the known price would be many lives.

There were dozens of craters at the top of Pointe-du-Hoc, maybe 50 feet across and 20 feet deep. These craters were created by the Allied bombs that blasted away at the German gunnery placements prior to D-Day. I stood above the cliffs and looked down 100 feet to where American Ranger battalions came to shore in the dark, before sunrise D-Day morning. The Rangers brought with them special guns that shot ropes and hooks to latch onto the top ledge of the cliff. They then began scaling the cliff as the Germans looked down from the top of the cliff and peppered them with bullets.

The vast majority of the Rangers died during this mission. Only a few made it to the top. Those that did make it to the top battled the Germans and forced them to retreat. This battle was critical to D-Day's ultimate success. Had the Germans been able to hold Pointe-du-Hoc, they would have been able to detect the invasion much sooner. I tried to imagine the selfless courage on display that morning. What did it feel like to be in that dreadful moment of truth, as the soldiers began scaling that cliff in the morning darkness, each ascending step taking them nearer to their deaths? For most, this would be the last morning, a morning that wouldn't include a sunrise. I tried to imagine, but could not.

We left Point-du-Hoc and drove to both the German and American cemeteries. The German cemetery was stark, the two cemeteries starkly different.

The American cemetery contained 9,387 tall white crosses set in perfect rows back and forth and diagonally. The green grass between the crosses was finely manicured. The setting was royal and majestic, looking out over the rolling blue seas of the English Channel. Several poignant monuments and statues were placed throughout the grounds in honor of the American soldiers who fought and died at Normandy. The American cemetery was both somber and breathtaking, a grand tribute to courage and lost lives.

By stark contrast, the German cemetery was hidden inland, away from the Channel vistas. The entrance was a small, dark portal that opened onto a flat, grim horizon. The German cemetery harbored more than 21,000 grave markers, all dark and set low to the ground, some appearing as short iron crosses, some appearing as flat grey stones. Several soldiers were buried side by side, acknowledged by a single marker.

In the center of the cemetery was a huge mound. Two black angels stood on top of the mound, back to back, facing opposite directions. Only when I got near did I realize what I was looking at: a mass grave for hundreds of unknown German soldiers. The German cemetery was, for obvious reasons, dark and subdued. That the French thought to honor their fallen enemy at all was an act of humanity during a time of such great inhumanity, and the establishment of the German cemetery was one of the first post-war acts of healing and forgiveness.

Adolf Diekman was buried in the German cemetery. Diekman was the SS Commander who ordered the massacre at Oradour-sur-Glane. Diekman made his way from the crime scene at Oradour only to die at Normandy in the post-D-Day battle. Some of us looked briefly for his grave marker but did not find it. I was interested to check my emotions had I been able to stand over his grave. Could I have been able to forgive him?

We came to the American cemetery and I braced to share my parents' story. Roiled with swells of emotion, I took a deep breath. The students and faculty gathered around me, standing together in a circle high on the bluff overlooking the English Channel. It was still winter in France, but this day was warm and beautiful. The sun was shining brightly. For the first time in months, most of us shed our heavier jackets in favor of sweaters, sweatshirts, and vests. Just as we formed our circle, the weather began to change. Slowly, the bright blue sky and water started to fade. A gentle fog climbed up from the sea to enshroud us. We could still see the first of endless row upon row of white crosses marking the American lives lost, but the fog otherwise held us closely and focused our attention.

There was a hush as I prepared to begin. This was a group of young people who had been strangers to me, and to each other, just a few short weeks ago. We had grown close during out time together. I was about to share the most personal of stories with them.

I began.

"As many of you know, I have been reading love letters written back and forth between my mother and my father during World War II. I want to share their story with you so that you can feel what it was to be like to be in the war, not from a historical perspective, but from a personal perspective.

"My parents were married just nine months when my father, 23 years old, left for the war. My mother was about your age. My father had no experience as he left home to captain an LCT landing craft. The ship was 114 feet long with a 32-foot beam and flat bottom designed for beach landings. The ship's purpose was to deliver soldiers, equipment, and supplies to the beachheads and to pick up casualties.

"My mother stayed home. Her concern was overwhelming, the tension unbearable as she waited for news. Was he wounded? Was he still alive? Would they ever be together again? When? She worried, tried to distract herself, and wrote letters of encouragement and support. Sending her love, it was all she could do. She longed for the future when this would all be over. But there was so much uncertainty how this would end.

"From my father's perspective, he was in hell on earth. He didn't want to kill anyone and he certainly didn't want to be killed. He was patriotic, but was not strongly engaged in the righteousness of winning the war. No one knew about the death camps or the other Nazi atrocities. My father simply wanted the war over with.

"The biggest weight that he bore was the inevitable responsibility for the wellbeing of the boys in his crew. Most of these boys were younger than any of you. My father wrote of how stressful it was for him to be in charge. His decisions and his ability to safely captain the ship would decide the crew's fate at Anzio, at Palermo, at Oran, and at Normandy—some of the war's most hotly contested and deadliest beachheads.

"Imagine how it felt to be bobbing in the waves and beaching the ship to deliver troops to battle. Imagine returning later with a Red Cross affixed to the ship's deck. The mission now was to pick up the dead and wounded men who you had earlier dropped off. The Red Cross was supposed to alert the enemy that this landing was a peaceful mission. However, it more practically served as a target mark for the German gunnery barrage.

"Ducking, dodging, laying low, fleeing were not possible. You simply carried out your business as quickly as you could and hoped it wasn't your time to die. As much as we want to believe in heroes, there were no heroes here. That's not the way the soldiers viewed themselves. It wasn't courage that was on display. It was mostly a collection of terrified boys and young men put in an impossible situation and reacting as best they could.

"Letters from home were so crucial to my father's morale. Sometimes the mail would get lost or delayed for days or weeks, which crushed my father's spirit."

I described the first air raid in detail, the precursor to more than 300 strikes that my father would live, but not to tell about. He never talked about the bad stuff. I told the story of the deadly torpedo strike that killed the ship's second in command. He never told me about that either. I spoke about the diversions that made some moments of this hell almost endurable—the dog mascot, Gertie from Bizerte, the bridge games, the sparse library of books traded back and forth at port during the war's peaceful moments.

Near the end, I pointed and asked the students to look through the fog out towards the English Channel—right there, right over there.

"Imagine a 23-year-old man who had been through all of this. Home was a world away. But that young man wanted nothing more than to be back home with his wife.

"Imagine that young man one night, a long time ago, floating in the darkness of the English Channel. You can almost make him out in the fog. Right there, right over there, that's where it happened. The invasion had passed and things were calm that night in the Channel. No one knew exactly how the war was going. The young man and the boys in the crew were hopeful, but uncertain. That night was like any other night. The ship was following the Navy's special operating orders for all ships situated in the Channel, no running lights and no radio communications. Audio and visual detection brought risk of German torpedo attack.

"Unexpectedly, in the darkness of night, the fleet commander's voice came over the radio, 'Sailors, resume normal operating procedures.'

"Stunned silence.

"A cascade of disbelief. A frantic search for comprehension. What? WHAT? Had they heard right?

"Yes, they had! It was safe to turn on the running lights, to use the ship's radio! Victory! The battle for Normandy is over!

"Imagine how it felt to have been through what these men had endured and to be on the deck of that ship that night. Imagine shouting at the top of your lungs and throwing your hats in the air. Imagine hugging your crewmates and pounding them on the back. Close your eyes and imagine the sight as my father and his crew threw the switch and turned on the running lights. Close your eyes and imagine the sight as all of other ships in the Channel followed suit. Imagine when, in my father's words, 'The entire English Channel lit up like a Christmas tree.'

"That was the moment when the war's end came into sight for my father, his crew, and all of the others guarding the Channel. 'We're going home soon boys.'"

I told this story with tears moistening my eyes and with a voice that I was somehow able to collect down beneath my lungs in the pit of my gut. I could tell by the tight-lipped, smiling, but tearful reaction of the audience that the story connected. It was a terrific feeling for me, to share my father's story with love, pride, respect, and admiration.

And so, in a matter of two days, I came to believe in God and to both forgive and love my father. I left home looking for a way to change my life. I had found what I was looking for.

Dogmatic Slumber

The American cemetery at Colleville-sur-Mer, Normandy

La Cambe— the German cemetery at Normandy

Gathering at the American cemetery, fog lingering over Omaha Beach to the right

CHAPTER 14
VISION QUEST

We returned from the beaches of Normandy to spend a second night at Bayeux. Bright and early the next morning we hiked to the guerre and boarded a train for a two-day stay in Amsterdam.

I hadn't spent time in Amsterdam before, though I'd heard a lot. I was looking forward to seeing what it was all about for myself. We stayed at a hostel near Vondlepark, Amsterdam's most expansive green space. I stayed with the students at their hostel rather than opting for the hotel upgrade, a lousy mistake. The hostel was noisy and filled with vagrant youths strewn throughout the lobby and lying on top of each other. At night they awoke and began running up and down the hallways loudly well into early morning hours. I'm not sure if God can witness, but if so, as God is my witness, I will never sleep in a hostel again. Plastic sheets, no more!

We arrived on St. Patrick's Day, a bacchanal in Amsterdam with throngs of boisterous beer drinkers and stoned pot smokers. A group of "elders," including myself, ducked the mounting party in the streets and instead had dinner at a decent Thai restaurant in the hood.

The Rijks Museum was closed for renovation while I was in Amsterdam. Similarly, the Van Gogh Museum was temporarily relocated with just a very limited display available for viewing. The line waiting to inside stretched around the block, rivaled only by the line waiting to see Ann Frank's house. Both lines were more than I wanted to take on, so I passed on both.

Given the circumstance, I made the best choice I could. I decided to see Amsterdam from the seat of a red, three-speed bicycle. *Ding! Ding!* I rented a bike and joined the herd. I rode shoulder to shoulder and head to tail within packs of dozens of other bicyclists. Avoiding crashes with my fellow cyclists, watching out for pedestrians, and dodging trams required all of my concentration. I was surrounded by native Dutch bikers who knew the ropes. They were going from Point A to Point B and knew exactly how to get there. I marveled at the city's spectacles, mostly lost and drifting without purpose and without regard for where I was or where I was going. I kept reminding myself to focus. I closely heeded the nearby bell alerts from my fellow cyclists. They were telling me that I needed to be aware, a point I wasn't going to argue. Though I gained confidence with time as I learned that bicyclists rule the road. It was the pedestrians who had the diciest lot in Amsterdam. *Ding! Ding!* Step back. Step aside. Watch out!

I rode through Vondlepark's gardens. Early flowers and trees were just beginning to bloom and bud. Children and families played on swings. I watched a few tennis points that a young woman won against her male opponent. They both laughed as she stroked her winners. I pedaled on past statues of what were, to me, unknown Dutch heroes, lakes, fountains, and an empty open air theatre.

I left the park and ventured out onto the city streets, past Rembrandt's home, through the crowded concrete of Dam Square, along the banks of the Amstel River, and into the bustle in front of the Centraal Train Station. People from all over the world were emerging from the station, launching themselves into Amsterdam's mix. I rode on further through many quiet and architecturally interesting neighborhoods.

One of Amsterdam's great neighborhoods was the Grachtengordel, a concentric ring of canals dating back to the 17th century. Central Amsterdam was mostly below sea level and made up of 90 small islands separated by canals and connected by bridges. The Grachtengordel was tidy and compact. Tall, thin, multi-story buildings, homes, shops, and restaurants lined its streets and canals. Most of the building roofs had crow-stepped gables ascending from eave to apex. Some buildings had large hooks placed high on the front exterior walls, hooks that were once rigged with ropes and used for hauling groceries several stories up from the street below.

I ventured into the red light district and walked my bike by the hookers. They were on display, confined to closets with street-facing windows. Looking upon their expressionless faces, it was difficult for me to imagine a person spending their life this way. More than difficult, it was impossible for me to imagine someone viewing the hookers from an erotic perspective. The buyers and the sellers were both pathetic, but the buyers clearly the more so of the two.

I enjoyed my limited time in Amsterdam, but I came away with an overall sense that the city was full of visitors looking for a good time, in search of a happy spirit that mostly eluded them. After two days in Amsterdam, it was time for the students to hit AbbeyROAD to Dublin, Rome, or Berlin.

My choice? I decided to travel to Ireland, both for the AbbeyROAD program and for my personal Vision Quest. So, early in the morning, I boarded a bus for Schiphol airport and headed out on my own. Once in Dublin, I planned to connect with Kevin, Jennifer, and Elizabeth, who were leading the curriculum for the Dublin group.

I stayed in a hotel located on Temple Bar, a lively pub district in the heart of Dublin. Temple Bar was just a block off of the Liffey River near Ha'Penny Bridge. The weather in Ireland was blustery and cold, complimented by a mix of heavy rain and snow. However, the traditional music, the food and drink (beefy Irish stews with turnips, sausages with garlic mash and brown onion gravy, oysters, and hearty Irish ales and Guinness), and the people—above all else the people—were warm and wonderful.

I spent most of my time in Dublin outside on my feet as soaked snow and slush fell from the sky. My borrowed umbrella from the hotel sagged beneath the weight. The streets were cold and windswept, but inside the pubs, the traditional music brought warmth and comfort.

I walked through St. Stephen's Green one day. In better weather, St. Stephen's would have been a striking park, with its extensive flower gardens arranged around the park's several ponds and small lakes. However, spring was still in the offing that day. It was cold, and any flowers that had emerged were sorry that they had.

I spotted a small pub, the Toner, and was happy to duck inside to get out of the cold. I was even happier to learn that the Toner had been voted Dublin's "Best Snug." The Toner's bar counter was worn and smooth, the vestige of the many patrons and tenders who slid shillings and mugs of beer back and forth over the ages. The pub's dark paneled wood walls were worn tatty by the timeless flow of music and crowds of laughter. The silver backings of the mirrors, the large mirror behind the barkeep, and the smaller ones lining the dimly lit booths once reflected shiny images. Those reflected images were now grayed and faded with time. But the music played and the beer flowed just as they always had in the Irish pubs.

The next night, I talked Elizabeth, Kevin, and Jennifer into going to the Church, a local recommendation for traditional Irish music. Formerly St. Mary's Church, the Church dated back to the beginning of the 18th Century. In more recent times, the Church had been converted to a restaurant and pub. The original high arching ceilings and massively ornate golden pipe organ remained, creating a sense of history and place that was palpable. Arthur Guinness, founder of the beer company, was married here in 1761. Jonathan Swift attended services at St. Mary's. And Handel practiced the Messiah on St. Mary's pipe organ before the oratio's first public performance, which was in Dublin.

There were two musicians playing together the night we were there. One played the fiddle and the other the Irish flute. The acoustics were splendid, and the two musicians filled the place with ancient sound, at times lively and at other times forlorn. The four of us snacked on pretzels and mustard, knocked back Galway Hookers, and absorbed the music as we laughed and talked about our lives.

Dubliners are proud of their writers—Joyce, Swift, Yeats, Wilde, Beckett, Shaw, and Kavanagh among others. There is something about Ireland's austerity, its poverty, its harsh and craggy land, the difficulty of family, and the constant religious strife. These elements have mixed together to create some of the most expressive writers to ever use the English language. Murals of their faces are painted on the exteriors of alley walls together with passages and famous quotations. Statues of them are ubiquitous, placed throughout Dublin's public squares, along the banks of the Liffey, and sitting on park benches. Dubliners celebrate these authors as if they were their very own sons and daughters. And in a sense, that is the case. All of the Irish share the same stories, mostly of want and pain. They share those stories with acceptance and indomitable spirit.

An interesting interlude was when Kevin and Jennifer arranged a discussion with a 70-or-so-year-old married couple, Mary and Des, who were friends of theirs. Mary had written a stage adaption of Joyce's *The Dead*. Des had spent much of his life analyzing Kavanagh's poem, "The Great Hunger," and was about to publish a book about his interpretation. Mary and Des wore their passion for Irish writers on their sleeves. They read passages to us in their distinctive Irish brogues. It was as if Joyce and Kavangah were in the room.

As much as I loved Dublin, the Ireland beyond Dublin was even more wonderful, perhaps as wonderful as any place I have ever been. Getting around Ireland was easiest through public transit, trains, and buses. Driving in Ireland was a wrong-side-of-the-road, white-knuckle affair, renting a car a go-at-your-own-risk proposition. Insurance was required and expensive, and rightly so. The roads were tight and twisted with barely enough room for the oncoming car, let alone the runaway bus coming around the bend.

Rather than drive myself, I twice opted for small tours leaving from Dublin, a one-day trip to the Ring of

Kerry and another one-day trip to the Wicklow Mountains. The tours were with small groups, five to six other individuals. The drivers were fun to know, told stories, and were armed with information and history about the area. I had no regret that I wasn't driving.

The Ring of Kerry was on Ireland's western coast, a spectacular circular route clinging perilously to the steep rock formations that fell away to the cold, rough sea below. County Kerry was made up of mountains, sheep, emerald green fields, and small villages, all belonging to an ancient time. Western Ireland was the land of the Potato Famine, a trauma which remains to this day as one of the most strongly flavored ingredients in the stew that is the Irish people. Western Ireland's fallow, rocky ground was just barely sufficiently fertile to subsist upon, and only then meagerly so with plenty of hard work and tough times, the way of the Irish. County Kerry was both harsh and beautiful, its people both tough and friendly.

The Wicklow Mountains were to south of Dublin, and my trip there moved me in a different way. The day itself was tough. Heavy rains and gale force winds pummeled us as we left Dublin. In Belfast, to the north, 40,000 homes were left without power. Rain gave way to snow as we approached the low-lying Wicklow Mountains. We were unable to clear the mountain pass due to the falling snow. However, we re-routed to the magical place called Glendalough.

The word Glendalough means "two lakes" in ancient Irish. The two lakes, an upper and a lower, flow gently into each other, the upper into the lower. The rounded

Wicklow Mountains slope down to the shores of both lakes, holding them tenderly in embrace. The lower lake drains out through a gentle stream that descends from the mountains and begins its long journey across the countryside, ultimately meeting and emptying into the Irish Sea.

A hermitic priest, St. Kevin, came to Glendalough during the 6th Century seeking solitude for religious meditation. The place was ideal, beautiful, remote, serene, and powerful all at the same time. What began as St. Kevin's solitary spiritual journey soon evolved into a growing monastery. By word of mouth, disciples heard about the grandeur of Glendalough. They travelled as pilgrims searching for this place, following the small tributary flowing from the lower lake. The sojourn was arduous, but the reward immense. Glendalough's tranquility was a special place to contemplate and perhaps find God.

The stream guided the pilgrims up through the mountains to Glendalough. Along the way, several stations were situated where the pilgrims could stop to rest, take shelter, and gain comfort with the knowledge that they were on the right path. The final pilgrim station was set near the shores of Glendalough's lower lake. It was a small, green, grassy mound covered with smooth, mossy rocks. An ancient stone Celtic cross, which has endured the elements for many centuries, stood resolute, marking the center of the mound, such a simple and elegant thing.

As I stood at the foot of final pilgrim station, I thought about all of the pilgrims who had travelled to this point. I wondered about them. Why was it that they chose to make such a difficult journey and what did it feel like when they arrived? Thinking about the pilgrims, I began to feel a strange sense of alertness, an awakening to something that should have been so obvious. They made the journey for the same reasons I was making mine. They felt the same way that I did. My decision to abandon my career, to travel abroad, to search, to quell a hunger that I could barely understand was culminating here and now at Glendalough. It was true. I had been on a pilgrimage of my own and I had arrived. Here I stood at Glendalough, where nature and God were undeniable. My pilgrimage was over. I had found what I was looking for. My Vision Quest was complete.

I returned from that day at Glendalough and packed my bags. Kevin, Jennifer, Elizabeth, and I were heading to Galway together the next day. The three of them had decided to rent a car to drive to Galway. I had planned to take the train, but they were heading my way so I bummed a ride. The three of them rented an apartment across the bay from Galway. I stayed at a small hotel near Eyre Square.

Galway was a smallish but lively town situated north of Kerry on Ireland's western coast. The lighthouse in Galway Bay was the last sighting of home that most Irish emigrants had as they boarded ships headed for America. JFK came to Galway shortly after his election. Kennedy addressed the loving crowd gathered at Eyre Square. The crowd cheered and cried. The people of Galway were so proud of him, one of their own, an Irish

Dogmatic Slumber

Catholic son returning home as President of the United States of America! To commemorate the day, the park at Eyre Square has been named Kennedy Park and a bust of JFK's likeness placed there.

Galway is also known for the Long Walk along the bay and the historic Spanish arches that open to the city. The culture, the traditional music, the woolen shops, and the food and drink in Galway are quintessential Ireland. The ancient Irish tongue is still prevalent throughout Galway and the western counties of Ireland. Musicians gather almost instinctively each evening at places such as Tigh Coili and Taaffes to make ancient sound. They make it together with their Irish flutes, whistles, wooden spoons, fiddles, squeeze boxes, uillean pipes, skin drums, banjos, bouzoukis, and mandolins.

Kevin, Jennifer, Elizabeth, and I drove north of Galway one day towards Connemara. Connemara, the very western edge of Europe, was a beautifully bleak, rough, craggy, and remarkable place. The landscape in places could have passed for the moon. Connemara was sprinkled with tiny villages with funny names, small homes with thatched roofs, khaki hills, slight mountains, unfenced sheep herds, and rugged coastlines. Connemara was a beautiful but desolate place. Few lived here. Those that did led simple, despairing lives.

I recall a conversation I had in Galway with a middle-aged woman who worked in a small clothing shop. She could tell that I was from the United States and gushed about what an absolutely wonderful and magnificent place America was. She had been there several times—New York, Las Vegas, Seattle, and Dallas, where her daughter lived. Next month she was returning to the States and had a layover in Chicago. She wanted to know what she should do in Chicago with her few hours of layover. America in this woman's eyes was such vast and overpowering place. "You Americans take such good care of your places and your historic sites. It's so exciting there. Everything is so poor and shabby here."

Her perspective struck me as odd. I tried to appreciate her view, but found it difficult. I asked her where she came from. She shrugged and told me that she came from a small village in Connemara. I asked why she left Connemara to come to Galway, a small town but probably larger than all of the villages in Connemara combined. She responded that there was nothing, no jobs and no future, in Connemara. She moved to Galway to take a job in this shop. I told her that Connemara was such a beautiful place in my eyes. She looked at me as though I were crazy.

I smiled and thanked her as I bought four woolen scarves, one for Laura, Audrey, Will, and me. In fact, I smiled the entire time I spent in Ireland. This woman, the people, the country were absolutely endearing. Everything that happened to me in Ireland boosted my spirit.

I loved Ireland and it was with regret that I boarded the train from Galway to Dublin and begin my journey back to Pontlevoy. I hated to leave, but at the same time I was looking forward to returning to my house in Pontlevoy and to reconnecting with the students. We had scattered in different directions for the AbbeyROAD and Vision Quest segments of their journeys, and I was eager to hear their stories.

I was also looking forward to a visit from a longtime friend, Ryan, who was coming to spend a week biking the Loire with me. Ryan lived in Seattle with his wife, Jan. Both were longtime friends going back to middle school, high school, and college. Our lives had gone in separate directions, and we had seen each other only occasionally over the years. Back in December, out of the blue, I sent Ryan an email to let him know that I was retiring and heading to France. Half in jest, I wrote that he had three choices: We could bike the Loire, travel to Ireland, or ski Chamonix in the French Alps. The choice was his.

This was a bit presumptuous on my part, but I knew that Ryan was at a point in his career where he had a lot of flexibility. He was a very successful attorney and business person who no longer needed to work for a living. I also knew that, like me, Ryan was a bit restless for adventure or something else. So it didn't surprise me when Ryan responded within five minutes of receiving my email that he'd prefer bicycling the Loire. "Let's do it," he wrote.

Ryan arrived the first week of April, a marginal month weather-wise. The week prior to Ryan's arrival had been fabulous, spring-like. I biked all over the valley that week basking in 50-degree-plus weather. However, the weather changed the week Ryan arrived. It got much colder, became overcast, and started raining. Boo.

We bundled up and headed out for our first bike ride in a cool but tolerable drizzle. We were prepared for the elements and had planned a fairly short 30–40 km route through the back roads down to the Loire by Chaumont and back up the hills to Pontlevoy. We were prepared and the ride was short, so we could handle the weather.

The ride did not end well. The reasons for the disaster were these: First, the rain intensified, the air temperature dropped, and our body warmth began to erode, not beyond what we could tolerate, but beyond the point where pleasure was possible. As we climbed the steep hill leading away from Candé-sur-Beuvron—*POOF*—the sickening sound of Ryan's tire flattening. Our teeth chattered as we dealt with the flat, pried the tire off the rim, exchanged the tube, twisted the tire back onto the rim, and inflated the tire with an inadequate handheld pump. Cold and sopping, we remounted, pedaling briskly to restore body heat. A couple of kilometers farther along the way—*POOF*—another flat for Ryan. Our cores were cooling, hypothermia was lurking nearby. Our fingers were cold and losing dexterity. And, due to my unfortunate oversight, our second spare was back at the ranch. Misery descended upon us.

I raced an hour or so back to the house to get the car while Ryan walked his bike slowly in Pontlevoy's general direction. He didn't have his bearings and didn't speak enough French to engage assistance. It was a miserably wet pedal home for me, a race through what had become nearly a downpour. Once home, I got in my car and drove to pick Ryan up. There were multiple

Dogmatic Slumber

routes he could be walking and I was glad to run upon him pretty early in the search. He was frozen and soaked. Moi aussi.

It was not the joyous ride through the countryside that we had bargained for. But in the end, once we got home, changed into dry clothes, cooked dinner, and opened a bottle of wine, the evening turned into a memorable one.

Here we were, two old friends who had gone separate ways but somehow ended up at nearly the same place at the same time. Like me, Ryan was searching. His career had taken him as far as he needed to go down that path. He wanted to do something else. I told him about my journey, about Terry, God, and the love I had come to have for my father. Ryan told me about his idea. Ryan was not particularly religious, but he did have a burning interest to research the facts surrounding the Bible and Jesus's life. Ryan wanted to establish a clear accounting, a separation of fact from fiction. He wanted individuals to have factually based information about the Bible and of Jesus rather than dogmatic interpretations based upon ignorance, hearsay, and blind devotion. We had plenty to talk about and went well into the night.

The next day was my turn for a bike breakdown. It was still cold, but no longer raining. We rode out along one side of the Cher and back on the other. Near the end of our ride, as we climbed the steep hill leading out of Bourée towards Pontlevoy—*CLANG*—my bike! I looked down. The derailer carrier had become caught up in the chain and snapped off. This was not reparable and not good. This time the misery, she was all mine. I walked with my bike up the hill towards home, a desolate six-kilometer march, while Ryan pedaled off to get the car. We met up about halfway along between the point of breakdown and home.

After that we had a couple of good, long rides. Ryan and I had been riding rented bikes. I ditched my broken rental and went back to my borrowed road bike. The weather was only cooperative to a point, still more like winter than spring. That said, we had a strong time of it, biking daily, rekindling our essentially dormant relationship, dining at a few local restaurants, eating cheese, fruit, and sausages at home, accompanied by an insurmountable volume of fine French wine. 2010 was indeed a very good year. I was able to introduce Ryan to many of the students, faculty, and friends I had come to make in the village.

I asked Ryan to lead a discussion with the Leadership Symposium on the topic of ethics. He did with aplomb and was able to tie his presentation back to Plato, a philosopher the students had been studying. At the end, I augmented Ryan's presentation with a story about him and me, a story highlighting the virtue of financial independence.

We were in Jamaica, 22 years old and vacationing with our wives. He was in law school and I had just received my graduate degree. Together we could barely put two nickels together. The four of us were hitchhiking around Jamaica, which saved us money but which was doubtlessly a bad idea.

An East Indian gentleman picked us up and told us that it wasn't safe where we were hitchhiking. He took us away and to his home in the mountains, where he owned pimento (all spice) groves. He served us coconut milk and rum on his front porch and told us a story, a story of chickens and eggs. "You see, young men, you can eat an egg for breakfast, or you can let those eggs turn into chickens. If you wait, one day you can have chicken dinners every night!" The story was a parable about the power of compound interest and how investments can work in your favor if allowed to do so. I told the students that my wife and I were affected by the story throughout our married lives. Whenever we thought about buying something extravagant, we would say to each other, "Sounds like an egg breakfast. Let's wait for a chicken dinner." And it was the truth. Living by that parable is what allowed me to retire early and to be with them today.

On Ryan's last day, it was raining—hard—with a daylong forecast for more of the same. We thought better of pursuing another misery-laden bike ride and instead decided to drive to Chartres to see its magnificent cathedral. Ryan could catch the short train ride from Chartres back to Paris and from there his flight home.

That morning, as we finished breakfast and prepared to leave for Chartres, I received the most unwelcome news that I have ever known.

Ring of Kerry

Road to Connemara

Dogmatic Slumber

Final pilgrim station at Glendalough

Glendalough—upper lake

With Elizabeth at Temple Bar—Dublin

Chapter 15
Henry

The message from Laura appeared unexpectedly on my phone:

"Please call when you can. Don't know if you have talked to Doug. Henry gravely ill and in hospital at U of W. Going into brain surgery this afternoon. Doug, et al. are at the hospital."

Henry was Doug's oldest son, the first of two. Henry was 21 years old and in his third year at the University of Wisconsin at Madison. Musically inclined, positively charged, very creative, and always smiling, Henry was that special type of person who could make others around him feel better, more joyful. He had a manner that created focused awareness of being alive and enjoyment of the moment. Henry, just like Doug, was life incarnate. This news, that he was gravely ill, wasn't possible. It made no sense. I refused it.

I immediately called Laura. The news was impossibly worse than I had imagined. Henry had gone to the University of Wisconsin hospital on Saturday night, complaining of fever, headache, and a racking cough. The medical staff examined him, determined that he did not have pneumonia, and sent him home. He felt poorly all day on Sunday. Monday morning he woke up feeling awful and walked back to the hospital. He was having difficulty speaking and one side of his body felt numb. While waiting to be admitted, Henry had a seizure and fell into coma. He had bacterial menegitis.

As I learned of this devastating news I searched for hope and next steps. However, I could tell from Laura's tone that hope was already being written out of the equation. The only next step was to wait. Henry's brainwave activity and responsiveness to external stimuli was being closely monitored, but was not encouraging. Surgery had been deemed futile and postponed. Family and friends gathered around the hospital waiting, waiting, waiting for a miracle. The clock was ticking and no news was bad news. The thin thread of hope that Henry would be able to come out the other side of this thing was under more strain than it could bear. As time passed, the prospect of Henry's recovery eroded and despair filled the void.

It was a horrible feeling to be so far away from Henry and his family, so powerless, sad, and confused. I hung up the phone and played the scenario back for Ryan. It was simply awful, but what could be done? At this juncture, only hope and pray. Ryan still had to catch his plane out of Paris the next day, so we decided to stick with our plan to drive to Chartres. I was obviously distracted with concern, concern metamorphosing to grief. When we arrived at Chartres, I was keenly aware, but tried to suppress the torrential flow of sadness within me.

We parked, got out of the car, had a bite of lunch, and walked to the Chartres Cathedral in the cold rain. The Cathedral in Chartres was magnificent with its immense flying buttresses and twin, asymmetrical gothic towers. Human statues of knights, kings, citizens, and monks, an infinite number of them, were carved into the cathedral's exterior design, particularly surrounding the cathedral's massive wooden doors.

But it was inside where the cathedral's beatific inspiration was truly on display. Brilliantly colored ambient light poured into the cathedral through a series of massive and exquisite stained-glass windows. The effect is divine. I walked through the nave and approached the altar sculpture, a heavenly alabaster marble depiction of L'Assomption. I felt deeply inspired to do something, something I had never before done in my life. I prayed.

With all of my being, with all of my love, with the entirety of might that I could muster, I prayed for Henry. I prayed for Henry to live. It was all I could do. I will never know if my prayers were heard. They certainly weren't answered. God did not intervene against the laws of nature to save Henry's life. But in an unexpected way, the act of prayer made me feel strong as opposed to powerless. The act of prayer, at least in my mind, rendered Henry a much more significant soul, a more enduring thing than the husk of human body lying motionless in the hospital bed.

We left the cathedral and drove to the train station. I remember Ryan's last words as he boarded the train: "I hope the best for your cousin's son." I thanked him, bid him safe journey, and turned away with tears in my eyes.

My solitary drive back to Pontlevoy was a blur except for one thing, the forceful internal dialogue almost shouting in my mind. "Come on, Henry! You can make it! Come on, Henry! Come on, Henry!" I drove alone across the gray French landscape, succumbing to wave after wave of faint hope overwhelmed by sorrow. I cried with abandon. "Come on, Henry! Come on…"

The next two days were miserable. The information available to me regarding Henry's status was inadequate and unacceptable. I received sporadic updates through email messages, texts, and Facebook postings, all of which were sketchy and slowly crowding out the remote areas where hope might still exist. I had a few sobbing phone conversations with Laura, with Will, and with Audrey; all so, so sad. Henry had no brain activity. Recovery was increasingly unlikely with the passage of time. A timeline was now being discussed as to when hope would officially be abandoned.

I lay in my bed, all to myself, for the better part of two days, both heart and mind empty of everything but sorrow. My thoughts echoed back and forth between so many things; so sad for Doug, for Henry's brother, Owen, for my son Will, who was like a brother to Henry;

so sad for Henry's mother and grandparents; so sad that Henry would be denied the great life that should have been his; so sad for Henry's friends and our entire family; so selfishly sad for myself to be losing Henry and perhaps a part of my cousin Doug that would never be the same.

I'm sure that I left my house more than once during these two days, but I only remember once. My house was set on a quiet stone street, just across from Pontlevoy's ancient parish church. Every Wednesday night, at a quarter to 6:00, the church bells would begin to toll. They signaled that it was time for the young boys to begin their walk from the nearby Catholic school to the church. As the bells rang, the boys walked happily together all dressed in uniform, khaki pants and red sweaters. They spoke in small groups and laughed as they wound their way through the streets and gathered inside the chapel. And at 6:00 they would begin to sing. The sound of their collective voice was angelic. I would often sit by the window in my house and listen to them, their sound heavenly, a ritual centuries old.

On this particular Wednesday as I heard the bells toll, I impulsively decided to go. I had never been to a worship service. I left my house, closed the gate, walked across the street, and tentatively entered the chapel. The chapel was dank and candlelit. The boys in their red sweaters were in front getting ready to sing. The church was about half full. I took a seat in an empty pew towards the back. I noticed a man alone in the pew in front of me with closely cropped hair. He wore sandals and an austere cloak, brown with a hood, and a long strand of well-worn wooden rosary beads draped around his shoulders.

The choir began to sing sweetly, divinely. The service was performed entirely in French and Latin. The words, sung or spoken, were difficult to hear and even more difficult to understand. But they sounded eternal and calming. I watched the man in front of me as he intensely obeyed the church rituals, which to me were mysterious. He stood, he kneeled, he crossed himself, he bowed his head, he raised his arms and hands towards the heavens. The man before me, the smell of incense, the angelic choir voices, and the chapel's antiquity came together to create a sensation that was foreign to me. I was uplifted and humbled. And I began to pray for Henry's life.

As I prayed, it occurred to me that perhaps my prayer would make a difference. I had an image in my mind of a scale that held Henry's life in the balance. My prayer, lighter than a feather, in fact weightless, might be the particle that was just enough to tip the scale in Henry's favor. Who knew? I prayed with all of my might.

It wasn't to be.

The next day Henry was taken off of life support and died. I couldn't bear this crushing load of sadness alone. I put on my coat, left the house, and went up the street to Le Commerce. There were several students gathered there watching a Champions League soccer match. All along, the students knew about Henry's circumstance but to my knowledge didn't yet know that he was dead.

Dogmatic Slumber

As I walked into the brasserie, things hushed. From behind the bar, Julien embraced me with unforgettable sadness in his eyes. I asked him what was up. He spoke solemnly, "Très désolé, so sorry for your loss." I was caught off guard. How had he heard? It was then that I learned that just moments ago Doug had sent the following message to the entire Abbey world.

"My dear students, your love and attention to my family and me means the world to us, even on a day that began my gentle boy's walk to forever. Henry's journey home began after lunch today here in Madison, with dozens of his adoring friends and family surrounding him with tender love and gentle tears. I thank all of you for your attention and affection. You would have loved my boy and he would have loved you."

Julien placed his hand on my shoulder, looked deeply into my eyes, and slid me a beer. "Gracieux." I looked across the room and saw the students, their eyes fixed on me. At that moment, the world stopped. One by one they came across the room and hugged me tightly with care and love. I realized then what I never would have imagined. I needed that from them. For me it was a powerful moment, a moment that I will always remember, when friends and faith helped me face an otherwise unendurable depth of sorrow.

That Sunday, the Abbey family held a Vesper service for Henry. The service was held in the Abbey Chapel. Terry Netter, SJ presided. The entire Abbey family attended—the students, the instructors, and staff—as did many village citizens.

A group of female students rendered beautiful songs acapella. Jennifer read "Farewell My Friends" by Rabindranath Tagore. Elizabeth read "Demain des l'Aube" by Victor Hugo. Kevin read an email that Henry had composed to console a friend.

Maddy,

I'm so sorry to hear about Tamar. I can't imagine what it's like to deal with that so far from home, but know that you're in my thoughts. Life is so fragile, but you are so strong, and although it would be easy to crumble in the face of tragedy, I know you will do no such thing. Of course, you will undoubtedly leave Galway a changed person, and although it's hard to say what will change exactly, you will most certainly be a bona fide adult. Scary, right? (I know...) What I'm getting at is something you already know; make the most of it, do what you want to do, and live a life of love and adventure. I am so lucky to have you as my friend, and so thankful for all the time we've had. So when you're at the pub after class, when the time comes be sure to raise a glass, to all future days and all days past, to friend and foe, all the people you know, and drink to good times and that long they will last. Miss you so much, Maddy!

I had the difficult honor of eulogy.

Eulogy for Henry Mackaman

Many of you never knew Henry Mackaman.

In Professor (Doug) Mackaman's words, "If you had met him you would have loved him and he would have loved you."

I want to talk about Henry and describe him to you so that, if you knew him, the description may help you remember him more vividly; and if you didn't know him, I want you to gain a sense for what kind of person Henry was.

No matter what, whether you knew Henry or if you did not, this passing of this 21-year-old young man, some 4,000 miles from here, has affected you. It has affected all of us. And why is that? It is because we have a shared experience here in Pontlevoy. And in this village a strong sense of community has evolved. As a result we have become closely connected to each other. And when one of us from our community experiences this level of anguish, we all feel it. We all want to reach out and let this person and this person's entire family know that we care. And it is important that I let you know that Henry's father and our entire family are aware that we're here right now, remembering Henry. They send their love and thank you for yours.

Henry died very suddenly and unexpectedly, and far too young. Henry went to the hospital a week ago yesterday with fever, head and body aches. He was released from the hospital after an x-ray showed no sign of pneumonia. On Sunday Henry felt somewhat better. But early Monday morning, Henry's friends took him back to hospital. He was obvious very ill. The situation quickly turned grave. Henry had a seizure and lapsed into a coma from which he never awoke. He died two days later of bacterial spinal meningitis.

So how does one reconcile that with anything that's comprehensible? With what is right, or should or should not be? I cannot. This time nature was very abrupt, random, and unforgiving. Henry's run on earth ended far too soon.

So, let me describe Henry to you.

Henry was a student. He attended The University of Wisconsin, where he was working towards a double major in Economics and English. He was on track to graduate with this diverse double major in just three years, which is remarkable. In the future, when you think of the University of Wisconsin, you should have kind thoughts. The University has announced that it will award Henry with a degree next month even though he fell one credit short of the school's graduation requirement.

Henry was very bright, a great student. He spent last summer in Compass Program, where he travelled Europe. He was a strong writer. In fact, he wrote and produced a play that was performed in Madison. Henry was clever. He made interesting word choices and was a wicked punster. Henry liked to look at things from different perspectives and see the world in new ways, perhaps in ways that no one else has ever seen it before. He was original and creative.

Let me describe Henry to you so that you can see him. He had a slender build and a boyish face. He had tousled, unkempt brown hair, which was never quite organized, but a look that suited him well. I will always picture Henry wearing jeans, tennis shoes, t-shirt, unbuttoned long-sleeved shirt over the t. He was and will be always smiling or laughing. It was his smile that is the most memorable part of Henry's persona. Henry was pleasant and agreeable. He made others smile.

What are some other words that I would use to describe Henry? He was such a sweet person. He was positive, polite, kind, and gentle. He was in no way aggressive, competitive, or angry. You never saw any glimpse of those things in Henry. No, Henry was the opposite of those things. Henry wanted everyone to be happy. Henry was a leader. People wanted to be around Henry. He had creative ideas. He was fun, playful, smart, and positively charged. Henry encouraged others to be interested, to be interesting, and to be their best. He owned the ability to touch people, to lighten them up. He could somehow engage people in a way that made them happier. Henry had a lot of friends! Many of them posted comments on Facebook or the CaringBridge website to the effect that Henry had a lasting effect on them, that they wouldn't be who they were today were it not for Henry.

I can't talk about Henry without talking about music. Henry LOVED music. I would guess that Henry would first and foremost have identified himself as a musician. He was an accomplished guitarist, composer, and producer. He co-founded the group Phantom Vibration, a very familiar band on the Twin Cities music scene. Henry played the guitar effortlessly and had a good singing voice. He was DJ on a student radio show that he hosted called "The Grooving Tree." He wrote a weekly blog on Murfie.com called "History Today in Music." All in all, Henry was a young but notable figure on the collaborative Twin Cities' music scene. This coming Friday night, there's going to be a musician's wake at O'Gara's Bar & Grill in St. Paul. I can tell you that all the cats are coming and they're bringing their instruments. It's going to be an incredible scene and a heartfelt tribute to Henry.

I need to tell you about Henry's family. Henry was surrounded by a triumvirate of three great families: the Mackaman family (Doug and mine), the Strands (Henry's mother Meredith's family), and the Ohara family (Henry's stepmother Maggie's family). In particular, I want to highlight the intense connectivity on display between three generations of the Mackaman family. Wayne and Dick Mackaman, my and Doug's fathers, respectively, were the very best of friends and loving brothers. Just recently, during the early part of the Abbey term, Doug and I were both laughing and sharing a few tears as we mused about how pleased and proud our fathers would be that we were so close and, like them, brothers. And then there's Henry and Will (Doug's son and mine, born a few months apart, both dear friends, and again like brothers). I remember the last time that I saw Henry. It was last fall in St. Paul. I was in town to visit my son, Will, to watch him play soccer for Macalester College. Henry was in town from Madison for a gig. That afternoon Doug and I rode bikes all over his beautiful neighborhood and up and down the Mississippi River. It was a great day, warm and sunny. The trees were electric with vivid fall colors. It was Doug's birthday. He, Maggie, Henry, and Owen went to dinner that night at Mancini's, a classic St, Paul steak joint. I went to Will's soccer game. He scored the winning goal. Henry's gig went well, despite the fact that he would always concentrate on the ways it could have been better. And I thought, "This is the way it should be! Life is good. Things are on track."

Well, I don't feel that way so much standing in front of you today. I should be going to Henry and Will's weddings and they should be going to my memorial service one day down the road. But that's not the way things have played out here.

Many of you have heard me or Doug mention Cedar Lake. I want to tell you about this place. My grandparents (and Doug's) settled an island on Cedar Lake near Aitkin, Minnesota during May 1915. This is a beautiful place with clear, deep, blue water, sweet-smelling green pine trees, loons and herons, and northern wildlife. And when the sun goes down, the sky lights up with stars, and sometimes, on magic nights, the colors of northern lights come alive. This has been the Mackaman family collecting point for nearly a century. Both of Henry's maternal and paternal grandparents, the Strands and Mackamans, built cottages on Cedar Lake. This was a place that Henry loved! He would swim there, play music there, fish there, swing in the hammock, watch and wonder at the stars, take saunas and then plunge off the dock into the cold lake waters, and join in the stories, laughter, and sometimes tears connected with his three great families. This is the place, more than any other, that has held the Mackaman family together. I spoke earlier about how abrupt and unforgiving nature has been. But Cedar Lake is where my family gathers to be with nature and to admire nature's incredible beauty. This is where we share and are reminded of our love for each other. Henry loved this place. This is more than a place. For our family, Cedar Lake represents everything that is good about nature, life, family, and love. Doug wrote me a note after Henry died in which he said, "Henry is in the arms of forever now, where peace and calm and Cedar Lake await us all." And that's the way I see it too.

Last, I want to tell you about Henry's final act as an organ donor, a courageous and kind act that will affect so many lives. Henry's favorite book as a young boy was "The Giving Tree" by Shel Silverstein. This is a story about a young boy who befriends a tree. He plays with the tree, climbing its branches. As an adolescent, the boy picks the tree's apples and sells them to augment his allowance. Later, as a man, he cuts some limbs from the tree to build a house. One day he chops the rest of the tree down because he needs the wood to build a ship to sail away. In the end, as an old man, he returns and falls asleep, resting at the stump of where the tree once lived.

The fact that Henry chose to be an organ donor is both courageous and kind, and I'm sure that this choice was impacted by his reading this book early and often at a young age. Because Henry made the decision to be an organ donor, shortly after midnight on April 11, seven people got the call that they'd been waiting for. An organ donor had been found and their lives would be saved. These people boarded planes and headed to Madison as quickly as they could. Almost another 70 people will ultimately have their lives significantly improved by the corneas, tissues, marrow, and so on that Henry had donated to them.

I want to close by sharing with you these words that Doug wrote and which were read over Henry's body as his life support devices were shut down and his life on earth ended.

"I am Henry Douglas Mackaman, born of Meredith Leigh and Douglas Mackaman in Oakland California, on 10 November 1991. I have lived a gentle life of music, smiles, friendship, family, and happiness. I died this week very rapidly after being attacked by bacterial spinal meningitis. I am leaving nothing behind on the table of this life other than the body you see here. Otherwise, I told my family and friends that I loved them. I learned. I read. I sang and played guitar. I saw a play of mine grow to be staged and performed. I watched World Cup soccer in Berlin, drank pilsners in Prague, and loved a girl over these last months named Margaret. The parts of my body that still work are yours now. I have no needs forever. I'm past the veil already and am even now with my own ones who left before me and have been waiting. While I'm also staying with my dear family and friends, from whom my leave taking will take their lifetimes to complete."

The following week, a memorial service was held for Henry in St. Paul. Both Will and I needed to be there for that. We made arrangements to meet up in Amsterdam to board a direct flight to and from St. Paul.

My journey began with an early morning train leaving Montrichard for Paris with a tight four-minute layover to catch a connecting train at St. Pierre des Corpes. The arriving train at Montrichard was late. There was no way I was going to make the connection at St. Pierre. There was only one flight out of Paris that was going to get me to Amsterdam and then St. Paul in time for Henry's service. I had to make that connection.

I jumped into my car and began racing to St. Pierre. I didn't know the route to St. Pierre, where to park when I got there, and had very little time to figure it out. With so much on the line, I raced along the Cher, flying over speed bumps and through roundabouts. Steve McQueen would have been proud. I rolled into the parking lot, grabbed my bag, ran to the platform, bought a ticket, and boarded the train, breathless, with only moments to spare. I was shaking with gratitude.

The remainder of the trip went well. Will and I met up at Schiphol, and together we crossed the Atlantic to say goodbye to Henry. Laura drove up from Des Moines to meet us in St. Paul. Audrey flew in from Seattle. We arrived at St. Paul and found our way to O'Gara's just as the musician's wake was beginning. It was an enormous crowd, the music an incredible tribute. The rush of family and friends greeting, hugging, crying, and laughing was overwhelming. I found Doug and hugged him closely, shouting over the music and through tears that this hug was from the entire village of Pontlevoy, a loving hug from so many friends who cared deeply for him and for Henry. His words were simple. "I need it. Thanks."

The memorial service the next day was powerful, filled with tears, remembrances, sadness, and beautiful human connections. Those gathered were the grandest group of loving family and friends as we shared both the love and the sorrow writhing in our hearts.

The next morning Will and I kissed everyone goodbye and boarded a plane back to Europe. It was, from one perspective, an exhausting journey back and forth across the Atlantic for just a weekend. From another perspective, it was the most powerful of family gatherings as we comforted each other, said goodbye to Henry, and together took steps forward towards a future that no longer included him.

One of the things I noticed during the trip back to the States was that I was seeing people, or rather they were seeing me, for the first time since some pretty remarkable things had happened. These folks, including my wife, knew me as I was before I'd left for Europe, not as I was now. I had changed a lot.

This journey back home brought into focus how I had changed. I had lost weight. I had not had a haircut for months. The short, practical haircut I had worn for most of my adult life had evolved into a shaggy, sweeping hair style. Will hardly recognized me and did a clear double-take when we met up in Amsterdam. The same went for Laura, who was stunned by my changed appearance.

I was smiling more, and many described me as though I were "radiating a glow," for lack of a better term. I hadn't expected it, but people were noticing a distinct change in me.

I had a few close conversations with family members about my experiences, the centerpiece being Terry Netter and my newfound belief in God. The reactions were interesting and varied considerably.

I had a thrilling conversation with my sister Ruth, unlike any conversation I've ever had with her. Ruth is absorbed with Yoga and eastern theologies. And it seemed as if we were talking about the same thing when, for the first time in our lives, we talked about God. She patted her chest as she told me that "God is right here," meaning close to her heart.

My cousin Craig seemed earnestly interested in our conversation about God. He and I had certainly never talked about God or religion before. He told me, "I'd like to talk more about this when we can," from which I sensed that he was perhaps open and had the desire to explore some of the ground I recently gained with Terry's help.

My sister Sarah, a dogmatic atheist, was entirely different and honest. From across the table she shouted, "Why, David? Why?!" from which I inferred that she felt as though I had somehow betrayed her.

My wife Laura, a devout Lutheran, questioned how a man I just met had convinced me to believe in God whereas an unending number of conversations throughout our thirty-plus-year relationship had not had that affect. That was a fair question.

Henry

Altar sculpture at Our Lady of Chartres Cathedral

Chapter 16
Leaving Pontlevoy

My weekend return to the States was a whirlwind. In just a few short weeks I would be leaving Pontelvoy and the Abbey to meet up with Laura and Audrey in Amsterdam. The thought of the ending began to close in around me.

Those last two weeks were filled with warm, spring-like days. Flowers sprung from the soil. The bike rides were warm and wonderful. One warm and sunny day I led a group of students on a ride. Our assembled collage of borrowed bikes performed unevenly, but we had a terrific time pedaling together. The students had not been able to range out much across the plateau's countryside. We laughed and smiled as we rode in the sun along the narrow one-lane country road to Candé-sur-Beuvron. As the weather warmed, I also played tennis with one of the students. She was considering making a run at joining the USM tennis team next fall, and it was fun to hit balls with her on Pontlevoy's public tennis court.

The end meant that it was time to wrap up the Leadership Symposium. While the symposium was ungraded, there was a final exam constructed upon the themes of storytelling, self-awareness, and personal development. I asked each student to prepare a response to the question that they would undoubtedly be asked when they went home: "So, tell me about your study abroad experience."

The purpose of the exercise was to help the students tell a tight, engaging story. I challenged them to think through in advance of being asked that question. What happened to you here? What was the most important thing, the thing that belonged as the centerpiece of your story? What words would you use and how could you say them such that people will to take notice of you and understand that you are an engaging person with fascinating things to say?

In the case of a parent, this story should be convincing that the time and money spent was well worth it. In the case of a potential employer, this story should put them on notice that your experiences were unique and that you developed life skills that would transfer into your being a better employee. In the case of your friends, this story should be compelling and entertaining.

I also asked the students to describe their individual Vision Quest journeys. Why did they choose their respective Vision Quest journeys? Describe what happened. Was there anything that surprised you? Why was the journey important? What did you learn about yourself and in what ways are you different for having undergone the journey?

The assignments were ungraded, but as we went around the room, there were nothing but A's. They all shared their stories loud and proud, each story heavily laden with vivid description, personal impact, self-awareness, and personal development. I was so proud of them all. Kevin, Jennifer, and Elizabeth sat in on the final exam, listening to the students, cheering them on as they each described their personal journeys. There was no doubt; the students had all grown as individuals and also grown together as a tight, caring community of friends.

After the students finished sharing, Jennifer turned to me and asked me to tell my story, the story that I would share when I returned home.

My story went like this:

"I had so many fantastic experiences during my time with you all at the Abbey: meeting new people from all over the world, now friends for life; tasting fresh pastries, cheeses, and wines; bicycling all over the Loire River Valley; visiting historic places; seeing some of the world's most inspired artistic masterpieces. I practiced my French. I saw both good and evil. I visited the Normandy Beaches where my father captained a landing craft in the war nearly 70 years ago. I read all of the love letters written back and forth between my mother and my father while he was away at war. I came to see my father in a different light, a light that caused me to understand him, to love him in a way that I never had before.

"I travelled to many different places: France, England, Ireland, Belgium, Germany, and the Netherlands. I learned and I taught. I grew both younger and wiser.

"I met a man named Terry Netter, a former Jesuit priest who changed my life forever. Before I met Terry, I had never believed in God. Terry helped me consider God's existence from a different perspective. I now believe in my heart that there is a God. That awareness has brought a sense of calm joy and purpose to my life. Love, beauty, kindness, and compassion have become priorities for me from here on out."

I described Glendalough to them, the twin placid lakes and the final pilgrim station. And I told them about the epiphany that came to me at the ancient Celtic cross marking the pilgrim station. I had been on a pilgrimage of my own and it ended there.

I told my story, circled by the students. They were clearly listening politely and, I believe, intently. One thing I will always remember for sure was a sweet young girl in particular. As I finished, she wiped a tear from both eyes and said in her sweet southern accent, "Now I will have something to cry about when I go to bed tonight."

That night marked the end of the Leadership Symposium. My time at Pontlevoy was likewise nearing conclusion. I was meeting Laura and Audrey in Amsterdam in just a few days. From Amsterdam the three of us planned to briefly visit Will in Groningen before spending a few weeks moving through other parts of the Netherlands, Belgium, Northern France, and England.

On my final night in Pontlevoy, the teaching staff and I packed into the Abbey's dilapidated old minivan and drove to Terry's home outside of St. George. He was hosting a potluck farewell. We stopped along the way at the Super U in Montrichard and loaded up with all sorts of cheeses, wines, a roast chicken, fruits, rosette sausages, and pâtés. The feast was flavorful, as was the celebration of the end of the term and the friendships we had kindled.

At the end of the evening, I hugged Terry goodbye. He had a gallery showing in New York planned for this coming November. I told him that Laura and I would move heaven and earth to be there. But who knew? We might not make it. Something might come up. Also, Terry was 84 years old and still struggling to regain his health. He still had that wracking cough that had plagued him all winter and into spring. Though I prayed not, this could be the last time that I ever saw this man. I hugged him dearly and thanked him for his friendship and for the change in my life that he had helped bring about.

We left Terry's home, shouted our final goodbyes, piled into the van, and headed out onto the dark country road to Pontlevoy. Elizabeth was our designated driver. She drove the van along the Cher and crossed the bridge leading to Montrichard. It was dark as we climbed the steep hill leading out of the valley from Montrichard. Ahead we could tell that something was amiss. The road was ablaze with brightly flashing police lights. There was a serious accident, most likely a deadly one gauging from the car lying upside-down in the ditch beside the road. The road was closed and we needed to find an alternate route. I knew my way around all of the back roads, since I had covered most of them while touring the region on bike. I directed Elizabeth down towards Bourée and a back road leading from there back to Pontlevoy.

The road from Bourée to Pontlevoy had no traffic and was pitch black. As we climbed the hill leading out of Bourée, we crossed the intersection of two dark, empty roads.

Suddenly the van's headlights went black. The engine stalled. We coasted to rest a few hundred feet in the dark middle of nowhere. The situation was disorienting, but I had our bearings. It was a six-to-seven-kilometer walk from there back to the Abbey. We pushed the van off to the side of the road and began trudging through the indiscernible darkness. It was late and there were no other cars on the road. The few scattered farm homes along the way were dark and had been that way for several hours. The only choice was to cover the ground on foot, step by step, not the way any of us had hoped or expected to end the evening.

Our physical fitness had a wide range, as did our shoes' suitability for walking. Completing the hour and a half walk was easier for some than others. But we kept our spirits as high as possible by telling jokes and stories. Gradually, the vague lights of Pontlevoy appeared on the horizon. With time, we narrowed and finally closed the gap. We ultimately arrived safely and in relatively good humor.

Everyone except for me was staying for another few days. I was leaving early the next morning. This was my last night. When we came to the Abbey gate, we stopped to say goodbye. I hugged each of them dearly, wished them well, and pledged to stay in touch. We were all strangers just a short time ago. Now we shared an experience and a genuine sense of warmth towards each other. I told them that I hoped to see them all again down the road. I said that, but knew that most of us would never find ourselves on the same spot on the same road again.

Having said goodbye to the teaching staff, I also needed to say goodbye to the students. I knew that they'd be celebrating the end of the term at Le Commerce. It was now well past midnight as I walked over to the small public square just outside. I was right, a couple of them were outside getting fresh air while the rest danced and laughed inside. I spoke to each of those standing in the square in as inspiring of a tone as I could muster that late into the evening. I told them how much I had enjoyed my time with them and about the amazing transformation I had witnessed in each of them over the course of the past few months. Those who had been inside came out to say goodbye. I hugged each of them, told them sincerely that I would miss them, and wished them well.

For me, these goodbyes were all very moving. I had not come to France expecting to cultivate close relationships with the students. This was a group of young individuals from a different generation, a different place and time than from where I came. We had little in common. But it did happen. Those relationships did evolve closely. I had come to know and love these kids, each in a different way. We marked the end of our time together with big hugs. We laughed as we hugged, but we also had a few tears in our hearts. No one wanted this to end.

I smiled as I said, "Revoir, mes amis," to all of them. I waved, turned my back, and walked alone down the dark, quiet rue to my home.

My rental house had become my home, and I was sad to be spending my last night there. I unlocked the courtyard gate and door. By now I was a master of both. Climbing the stairs for the last time, I turned out the lights, fell into bed, and lay alone and awake for quite a while, reliving my time at the Abbey.

My bags were already packed. With eight hours of driving ahead of me, I needed to leave early the next morning. My plan was to drive to Groningen in time to catch one of Will's soccer matches. I wasn't staying in Groningen, but driving on to Amsterdam so that I could meet Audrey and Laura's planes the following morning.

The next morning I woke up, got dressed, walked down the stairs with my bags in hand, climbed into my Renault, and backed out of the courtyard through the gate onto the street. I parked on the side of the street and went to swing shut the courtyard's massive wooden gate with a creak and a slam. I got back in the car and looked over my shoulder at the Abbey, which was still asleep. Dawn was just beginning to break. Easing down La Rue de Colonel Filloux for the last time, I turned right past the grade school, made an another right along D764, and accelerated along the small country road heading towards Blois, Paris, and beyond. I was on my way.

This part of my journey was over. I had expected to feel a sense of emptiness, or some sense of loss, of finality, of sadness as I departed. I did, all of those things. However, as the village slept and as I pulled away and headed out of town, I also felt a sense of completion. My time in Pontlevoy had been one of the most remarkable times of my life, but nothing lasts forever. It was time to leave.

Leadership Symposium—chez moi

Vision Quest storytelling

CHAPTER 17
WTF (With the Family)

I had a fair amount of ground to cover: 850 kilometers to Groningen for Will's soccer match and another 200 kilometers from Groningen to Amsterdam. I took full advantage of the auto route's 130 km speed limit, arriving in Groningen about an hour before Will's match. The match was a friendly against the Ajax alumni team, the Ajax being one of the world's most venerable professional soccer clubs. It was an honor for Will to be on the same pitch with these former players. I was looking forward to the match.

It was bigger and better than I could have imagined. There were young men from Will's club, GASVV Forward, selling admission tickets to the match for 10€. They recognized me as the American player's father, were expecting me, and welcomed me warmly. I bought a ticket and joined the large, boisterous crowd.

Will played well. The 1-0 score in favor of the Ajax didn't matter much. Everyone was having fun, particularly the large section of young men drinking beer, chanting and singing soccer songs and cheers, banging drums, blowing horns, and lighting flares and smoke bombs. There was a brave streaker who made his way around the entire perimeter of the field. And there were two voluptuous beer maids dressed in royal blue "uniforms" promoting Bavarian Beer brand. Sales were going quite well that day. The Dutch take their soccer straight up and celebrate seriously.

I greeted Will after the match and could tell from his face that things were going well for him and that playing soccer with a European club was one of the highlights of his soccer playing days.

After the match, I said goodbye to Will and drove another two hours to Amsterdam. I stayed at a fleabag near the airport and got up early to first meet Audrey and then Laura. It was a special day, April 28, Laura's birthday! I met Audrey's plane first and a little over an hour later, Laura's. We all hugged and kissed each other, gathered bags, jumped in the car, and headed north to Groningen to meet up with Will. That night we celebrated Laura's birthday at one of Will's favorite restaurants, Italian, one of the few restaurants he could afford on an occasional basis. The four of us together—in Europe, after so much time apart, on Laura's birthday—life can be so good.

One of the things we talked about at dinner was my experience at the Abbey. Audrey and Will asked me to tell them about it. What was it like? So of course I told them all about it. Odd to say, but I was uncomfortable talking about the centerpiece of the story, my newfound belief in God. I don't ever recall a conversation about God with either Audrey or Will. I told them about Terry, the moment of truth on the bus ride to Bayeux, and about the new, loving, respectful relationship I now had with their grandfather. In a way it felt like I was having a talk about the birds and the bees, although we never had that talk either. This was a serious conversation about something we simply didn't talk about.

For me the conversation was awkward. It shouldn't have been but it was. For Audrey and Will, I'm not sure. I'm sure they were surprised that I ever held anything in my heart but love for their grandfather. That's all they ever held. Regarding God? They seemed to be listening and processing. I didn't ask them what they were thinking and they didn't tell me. Right or wrong, I have always felt that people need to figure out things like faith on their own rather than to be instructed by their parents. Religious instruction is where the seeds of dogma are sewn.

The next day we explored Groningen as a family with Will as our guide. I'd spent several days in Groningen earlier, but it was really a new frontier for me. Back in January, when Will and I were in Groningen together, it had been cold, dark, and charmless, principally because we had neither our winter coats nor a change of clothes. Now it was spring and Will had learned his way around.

We visited Will's Spartan one-bedroom dormitory room, which was tucked away in a quiet neighborhood.

We wandered the Grote Market streets, climbed 260 spiral steps to the top of the Martinitoren Tower, and walked along the canals filled with barges, tugs, skiffs, and houseboats. We met some of Will's friends at Noorder Plantsoen, a sprawling green park located near the city center. It was a warm and sunny afternoon and the park was alive with throngs of students from the University. We hung out, talked, and people watched as the students played Frisbee, listened to music, and sat on blankets in the sun. It was a day for fun, no worries in this place on the planet.

For my money, Groningen was a much more endearing place than Amsterdam. Will's mother agreed. But she was horrified to learn that there was a small red light district in Groningen, worse yet that her son knew where it was. Laura did not take Will up on his offer to show it to her. In any event, it was clear that Will was having a grand experience and was gaining independence. He was learning a lot in the classroom pertinent to his major. As important, he was learning a lot about himself.

We spent two days in Groningen, which included a drive through the Dutch countryside and several small villages along the North Sea and the German border. On the morning of the third day, it was time for Laura, Audrey, and me to move on.

We were sorry that Will couldn't come with us, but he had school commitments. Even more important, it was Koningsdag—Queen's Day! Will and his friends had big plans to celebrate, which I'm sure they did, along with the entire Dutch population. We hugged Will goodbye and headed south towards Amsterdam and beyond. Will went back to bed to rest up for Queen's Day. The celebration promised to last all night long.

I was completely unaware of Queen's Day until we were there in the middle of it. It's a huge thing in the Netherlands, where it ranks as one of the most anticipated holidays of the year. As the name implies, this is the day when the Dutch celebrate their Queen. This particular Queen's Day, 2013, was extra special. Queen Beatrix was retiring from the throne and her son, Willem-Alexander, was stepping in. The "Return of the King" was a big deal across the entire country—orange balloons, orange flags, orange wigs, orange hats, sweaters, and pants, orange banners, orange, orange, orange everywhere; and beer, beer, beer everywhere as well. Celebration ran amok.

The population of Amsterdam grew by two million on Queen's Day as revelers travelled there to revel. We steered well clear of the Amsterdam celebration. However, we did stop at Keukenhof Gardens outside of Amsterdam. Holland is known for tulips, and Keukenhof—a massive and surreal explosion of color and fragrance—was all about tulips. Keukenhof was spectacular row upon tidy row of alternating brightly colored flowers. There were more tulips than you could shake a stick and all exactly placed. Glorious, but also a somewhat puzzling commitment to a flower that bursts momentarily into bloom for just a week or perhaps two before retreating into dormancy. In any event, the tulips were joyous that day. Yes indeed, we enjoyed their uncommon beauty before moving on to Bruges in Belgium.

We rented a 17th century, Flemish, three-story house in Bruges, "The Lady of Lace," near Bruges's Market Square and the Belfry Tower. Bruges was an impossibly quaint medieval village, preserved as if it were a living museum with its bell towers, narrow winding streets, ancient cathedrals, and ever-present canals. The place was charming almost to a fault. The most decadent chocolate, the most delicious waffles, the most intricate lace, and the most splendid beer in the world were all legion in Bruges.

On our first morning we went to farmer's market in the Market Square to buy things to make dinner at home that night. Audrey is vegetarian, so we loaded up on fresh vegetables, cheese, and pasta. I took a picture of Audrey eating a caramel-smothered Belgian waffle in the market. She looked as though she was leaving her body, pure ecstasy.

While we were at the market, somewhere between the carrots and the squash, the crowd parted. Unexpectedly, the oompapa of a marching band stormed in to fill the void. The band was a couple of dozen men and women strong, all dressed in black and white uniforms. Two lines of drummers led the way, followed by a line of tuba players, trumpeters, flutists, and so on. The band marched into the square unannounced, passed through the crowd, and exited the other side of the square. They turned left as their muffled sound gradually faded away. As it turned out, this band marched perpetually, all day long, through the streets of Bruges. We would later encounter them several times and life would always come to a standstill until the noise passed. We agreed that seeing them once was enough.

We left Bruges after two days, driving onward north to Ault, a small seaside French village on La Manche, the English Channel. En route, we stopped at the World War I Museum in Ypres near Belgium's border with France. Some of history's grimmest, most horrific battles occurred at Ypres, hand-to-hand combat for control of "No Man's Land," the barren patch of mud and dirt lying between trenches hand-dug by opposing armies. The battle was waged with gruesome instruments of war: mustard gas, flame throwers, landmines, machine guns, mortars, grenades, and rifles tipped with bayonets.

Many of these weapons had just been invented and were being newly tested in the arena of war. Hooray! They worked. These weapons induced blindness, mutilations, amputations, and death at a rate that clearly outpaced the development of medical treatment. The human collateral damage was shocking and unprecedented. Half a million souls were lost at Ypres during World War I. Our collective memory of these things and the brutality of World War I have faded with time, eclipsed by more recent and more modern manners of waging war.

Visiting the war museum at Ypres reminded me about World War I's unrivaled brutality. It also reminded me about all of the things I had seen during my time at the Abbey. I had seen layers of history often defined by the violent struggle between good and bad, between compassion and aggression, between the purportedly pious and the blasphemous. Here we were again, more of the same. There must be a reason for this endless tension between cruelty and kindness. Who could argue that kindness is not the better of the two ends of that spectrum? Perhaps cruelty and suffering are the motivation and the fuel for future acts of kindness? Perhaps suffering is what causes us to grow stronger, more resolved. Who knows? But a trip to Ypres begged these questions and more.

From Ypres we drove across the French border to Ault, in northern France, where we rented a top-floor seaside flat. Ault is a small coastal village perched on a steep cliff overlooking the Baie de Somme. The cliffs on the French side of the English Channel were steep and dramatic, similar to the Cliffs of Dover on the English side. Ault was very quiet. The few indigenous restaurants served simple but "oh so fresh" seafood. The boulangerie next door was out-of-this-world in true French fashion. During summer the beach in front of our flat would have been filled with people playing in the sand and swimming in the surf. It was early spring when we were there, and instead the beach made for quiet, peaceful walks.

We hiked the cliff-hugging trail from Ault to Bois de Cise, perhaps five or six miles roundtrip. Bois de Cise was a tiny and serene village, tucked into the Somme's hills and woods at the end of a small road leading to nowhere but there. Victor Hugo, Jules Verne, and Colette escaped summers in Paris and came here to write in the region's breezy solitude. Hugo in particular spent time at his summer home at Bois de Cise.

While walking we came upon a small brown chapel in the woods, Chapelle St. Edith. The church had special meaning for us. My mother's name was Edith.

The chapel was quaint and idyllic…that was, until you went inside. Inside we found a larger-than-life mural of St. Edith bearing an uncanny resemblance to my mother. She was smiling sweetly, but incongruously wielding a bloody ax. Legend has it that the virgin St. Edith singlehandedly fought off a group of invaders with an axe. She saved the village, an act of valor that qualified her for lower level sainthood. As I gazed upon the mural, focusing on the bloody ax, I had an image in my mind of St Edith standing over the slain marauders and consoling them with my mother's classic line, "Well if that's the worst thing that ever happens to you…"

After three days in Ault, we packed up and drove west to Calais, where we boarded a ferry crossing to Dover. The crossing took about 90 minutes. We were exhilarated as we drove onto the ferry with the destination the Cotswolds of England. We were even more exhilarated, no panicked, as we disembarked at Dover and were immediately launched into traffic coming at us from the wrong side of the road.

We managed the drive from Dover to the Cotswolds safely, maybe a six-hour drive allowing for stops in the towns of Rye and Hastings along the way. Our destination was the village of Bibery, a picturesque village about two hours west of London where we rented a cottage for the better part of a week. The essence of the Cotswolds was rural and enchanting in an old English way. The region featured small village pubs, sharp stiltons, cheshires, and cheddars, red roadside telephone booths, and glorious country walks. The Cotswolds were sparsely populated with quaintly named villages, each worthy of their own postcard, villages such as Stow-on-the-Wold, Chipping Campden, Gloucester, Winchcombe, Burton-on-the-Water, Tetbury, Moreton-in-Marsh, and Cirencester. All of these villages were connected by small rural roads wending tightly through the pastoral countryside.

The country walks were marvelous, lightly tread pathways over hill and dale, through woods and pastures, along streams, and over stone walls with stiles. It was the country walks that most distinguished the Cotswolds for us. The English have placed great effort on coordinating private land ownership with public access such that everyone can enjoy these naturally inspiring walks in the country. We walked almost every day, for hours. Traversing the countryside on foot brought us into the palm of a beautiful serenity.

We were fortunate enough to time our stay with a weeklong classical music festival held in nearby Chipping Camden. We made a great choice by deciding to attend an organ performance by John Scott Whitely. Mr. Whitely was organist emeritus of the York Minister, a fanatical Bach organ expert, and purported to be one of the world's most accomplished classical organists. His performance that we witnessed at the ancient Wool St. James Church did nothing to belay his reputation.

Dogmatic Slumber

The antiquity of St. James, which dated back to the 15th century, combined with the complex genius of Bach and the thundering sound of the church's enormous pipe organ, brought together both the appearance and the sound of divine inspiration.

The Cotwolds were also known for their wondrous and mystical stone circles, Stonehenge and Avebury being two. Stonehenge was awesome and unimaginable in the true sense of those words, but also somewhat unapproachable. We could only view Stonehenge from a fair distance. Its stones were fenced off for protection, whereas we were able to walk right up to and touch the stones at Avebury. Avebury was not as architecturally complex as Stonehenge, but was older than Stonehenge and dwarfed it. A mindboggling circle of gigantic stones, Avebury was more than a quarter mile in diameter, fully encircling what was once an ancient village. Avebury's stones were huge, some weighing in excess of 40 tons.

Nearby was another monolith, Silbury Hill. Silbury is a Neolithic monument, a manmade mound standing 130 feet high, seemingly in the middle of nowhere and for no known reason.

It all caused me to wonder. Seeing the achievement of Stonehenge with my own eyes; looking out at the manmade mountain of Silbury; feeling Avebury's ancient mystery with my own fingertips, standing beside the immensity of the stones towering over me—I wondered, how and why were they here? These things were done on an unworldly scale, no doubt inspired by someone's desire to relate to God.

We also went to the Berkeley Castle. The Magna Carta was drafted at Berkeley in 1215; King Edward II was murdered there in 1327; and Cromwell breached its walls during the civil war in 1645. A small story about Dickie Pierce, the court jester at Berkeley, was my personal favorite.

I had come to appreciate the sad existence of court jesters ever since I visited the Don Jon at Loches, France. The Duke of Milan was captured and imprisoned at Loches. Out of respect for his loyal position, the Duke was allowed companionship of his jester, whose job was to keep the Duke constantly entertained. What did the jester ever do to deserve that?

In any event, the story of the jester at Berkeley dates from the 14th century. His name was Dickie Pierce. Dickie, by all accounts, was a wonderful jester, well-liked by all. One night Dickie was entertaining from the elevated minstrel's gallery while the nobility watched from the dinner table below. Dickie's trick de jour was to roll himself into a ball in such a way that the dinner guests could kick him around the room. Sadly, the participants got a little too rambunctious that evening and accidentally kicked Dickie over the balcony's edge. He fell to his death, dropping upon the horrified dinner guests seated below. And, in the words of our tour guide, "That was the end of Dickie Pierce."

Our time in the Cotwolds was nicely flavored with old-world food and drink, long country hikes, and the remnants of an incredible expanse of history. I thought to myself about how I was taking in the experience. In the past it would certainly have been a delightful interlude, to be in Europe having fun with Laura and Audrey. But as I reflected, it was different now.

As I beheld the mystery of the stone circles, I did so in a way that I would not have been able to before. As the glorious organ music of Bach filled the space between the ancient walls of St. James Wool church, I listened differently. As I walked in the country, I heard the songbirds differently, and the sound of the passing stream, a stream that has flowed forever in the Cotswolds, differently. I was calmer, more contemplative, more appreciative, and more awestruck. I could see God wherever I went, in nature and in man's creations.

And then our time was up. It was time to go home.

We left Bibery early in the morning, fought through an unfortunate flat tire incident. A flat tire is never a good thing. Figuring out the spare tire mechanism for a French car made it worse. Trying to replace a French tire in rural England compounded the agony. "We don't sell French tires here. We only sell good tires," the man at the tire store in Cirencester told me. He helped us find the best match possible and we hit the road my pocket book 100£ lighter.

We stopped at the moated Bodiam Castle in East Sussex and spent our last night in England at Winchelsea before boarding the ferry back to Calais. We had a nice dinner together at Winchelsea Inn and walked about town, but we were in motion and our travel was evolving towards a mostly business affair.

We had a long day's drive the next morning to the ferry, the passage across the channel, and the drive from Calais to Amsterdam.

All the hassles of travel began to emerge once we got to Amsterdam, a one-night stand in an uninspiring hotel, non-delicious convenient food, early morning alarms, coordinating return of the car, making connections, clearing customs, saying goodbye to Audrey as she boarded her return flight to Seattle, and so on. For Audrey and Laura, it was the end of a great holiday. For me, it was the end of something much bigger.

Laura and I boarded our plane in Amsterdam. As the plane prepared to leave, I looked out of the window. There was no Gremlin on the wing this time. I quietly took inventory of all the things that had happened to me since I left home. I was going home a much different self than the one that had left. All of my bags were packed and loaded on the plane, except one. I left behind the bag that once held my dogma.

Will post-Ajax alumni match

Audrey posing with owl on Queen's Day

Laura and Audrey at Keukenhof Gardens

Bruges canal

Bruges market

Walk along La Manche from Ault to Bois de Cise

Ault seaside

Bois de Cise

Chapelle St. Edith—Bois De Cise

St. Edith!

Country walk—Cotswolds

Bibery Bridge

Avebury Stone Circle

Bodiam Castle—East Sussex

Dover

Chapter 18
Coming Home

As soon as we touched down at Chicago O'Hare, we rushed to clear customs. Our connecting flight was fairly tight. The line of passengers waiting to clear custom was endless and unmoving. We waited impatiently for our turn. For months I'd harbored a lingering concern about overextending my stay in the EU without obtaining a proper visa. That concern now moved from the back of my mind to the front. I wondered if I was going to get called out on that. I guessed that I was about to find out and wondered what the consequences might be.

I heard my mother's voice, "You mean for breaking the law? That will probably be the worst thing that ever happens to you. And you'll deserve it."

I hung my head and said to myself, "Thanks for that, Ma."

Finally, it was our turn. We approached the dour-looking customs agent. He, like most customs agents, lacked any visible sign of empathy. Rather, he exuded distrust and discontent. He was an older man with grey hair, a uniformed paunch, and the task of Sisyphus behind him. The line was infinite and growing. Everyone was in a rush, but not he. He was going to take his time and do this right.

We handed him our passports. He lingered over mine, a terrible sign. He held it up, looked at me, looked back at my passport, back at me, back at the passport and finally spoke.

"This guy in the passport is ten to fifteen years older than this guy." He pointed at me as he spoke the words "this guy." At that point, our conversation turned from the business of clearing customs to a jovial and pleasant exchange. He sincerely wanted to know what I had been doing that had caused me to now look several years younger than my passport photo.

"Seriously," he said, "I've been doing this for years and you are ten to fifteen years younger than the guy in this picture. Whatever, you've been doing, keep it up." He smiled and waved us through, so distracted that he failed to note my visa breach.

This was the first reaction I received upon my return to the States, an unsolicited reaction from a stranger. Whether it was because I had grown my hair out, that I had lost weight, that I had replaced stress with joy and was now smiling, that I had awakened from my dogmatic slumber and made the choice to believe in

Dogmatic Slumber

God, that I now loved my father, or, more likely, a combination of all of these things, I would come to hear this often upon my return. People would tell me that I looked younger. For lack of a better way to describe it, many friends would tell me that I had a "glow." And the most beautiful thing was that this was the way I felt. I was awake, joyful, appreciative, and humble.

Before I'd left for Europe, I had talked with a lot of friends, family, and business acquaintances. We talked over coffee, lunch, dinner, or a glass of wine. I remember one conversation in particular with my neighbor, Matt.

Matt, a biochemist, was much younger than I was. Over coffee I told Matt that I was leaving my job. Why? Well, among other things, I was looking to be healthier. I planned to eat better, to exercise more consistently, and to reduce the influences of stress and anxiety. Matt was intrigued with the entirety of our conversation. But, being the scientist that he was, he suggested that it would be fascinating if there were a way to empirically measure my health before and after.

Frankly, I didn't give Matt's comments a whole lot more thought until a few weeks after my return. I needed to complete a health screening exam for our insurance company. I had taken an identical exam two years ago, which made it a simple deed to compare my health before and after. I opened the envelope with my current results and set them next to the results from two years ago. Holy cats! I couldn't believe my eyes. The comparison was undeniably positive across the board.

Weight	Lost 10 pounds
Waistline	Shrunk 4 ½
Blood Pressure	Never a problem, but now 110 over 80
Body Fat%	Down 3.6 percentage points
BMI Index	Down 1.1 percentage points
BMR(kj)	Down 4.8% (whatever that was)
BMR(kcal)	Down 4.8% as well
Impedance (impedance not impotence)	Down 10%
Fat Mass	Down 7.8
FFM/TBW	Down/Down
Glucose	Up 14 (bigger is better)
Cholesterol	Down 29
Cholesterol HDL/LDL	Down from 4.2 to 2.8
Triglycerides	Down 23

These health measurements had always been fine for me, but they were now significantly improved. I had one area of concern. I wasn't seeing as well. I went to my ophthalmologist. I needed a new prescription... actually an old prescription, the one I used ten years ago. My eyesight was improving.

I couldn't deny it. Any way I could assess it, I had become a healthier man. I was not only healthier, I was happier. Or better said, perhaps because I was happier, I was healthier. I was more positive. I had regained energy and zeal, things that had slowly faded with age and with my growing discontent with the course of my life. I was more loving, more devoted to personal relationships with family and friends. I was more attentive, more appreciative, and more noticing of beauty. The effects of being happy were clearly manifest on my physical being.

Back home I was greeted by our English Labrador, Maya. We love and missed each other. Maya's a good dog. I tell her that every day. Shortly after I returned home, Maya and I went for a long walk. She smiled and romped through the woods. My thoughts roamed from this to that. I thought about what I had been through and what I had learned. I was healthier and happier. Was I any wiser for the journey? If I had to boil it down to one thing, what did I learn?

I thought about my friend, Terry Netter, and recalled a story he'd once told me. Terry was at the bedside of a dear mentor, a Jesuit, who was near death. The man had no remaining family outside of the church. Terry was his closest friend. They were exchanging final words and Terry asked his friend, "What do you think it all means?"

His friend paused, opened his eyes, and replied, "You've got to be kind, man."

If I hadn't learned anything more than that, that was enough.

Home with Maya

Epilogue

So what? What does this story mean? How does any of this matter?

Well, for one, I love to write, and the process of creating this book, of putting my experiences to words, has brought me great joy. If you too have a dream to write, I encourage you to do it!

For another, being forced to connect one event to another in the form of a story, to reflect upon the personal impact of these events and the emotions that they have stirred, to deliberate on the outcomes that have resulted from the choices I have made has been incredibly enlightening. The process of committing my thoughts and experiences to words has brought clarity. Every day we all experience so many things, beautiful, awful, banal, and otherwise. And so often we fail to take notice. We fail to register the impact. Writing this story has helped me take notice of what was happening to me and within me. We can all take better notice of the world both around us and within us.

For another, the human spirit is an instrument intended to play a wondrous melody. I awoke one day and found that my strings were taut and out of tune. I can't help but feel that many of us have inadvertently found ways to cope that gets us through but that also wrings much of the joy from life. I am not alone. Many of us have become too comfortable in our slumbers. Are we all equipped with sufficient wisdom early in life to make life and career choices that will maximize our joy, our passion, our purpose? The odds are long. But if we honestly pay attention to our inner dialogues, if we are clear about priorities and values, if we are purposeful in our choices and our self-development, if we try to understand situations from different perspectives, and if we are trusting and courageous enough to make the changes suggested by our intuition, by our life experiences, and by our close relationships, we can make midcourse adjustments that will make all the difference in the world.

And finally, you've got to be kind, man.

Acknowledgements

Laura, thank you for supporting me and for putting up with me through all of my endeavors, including the writing of this book. I love you.

Will, I love you too. Thanks for sharing parts of your study abroad experience with me. We had the time of our lives, didn't we?

Audrey, copy editor extraordinaire, I owe you a very special note of thanks. I am so proud of you. Your encouragement, support, and feedback kept me going and got me across the finish line of completing this book. Your expert advice has been invaluable. I love unicorns, Ulysses S. Grant, eucalyptus...and you.

Thank you to all of the instructors, staff, students, and villagers from Pontlevoy that I met during our time together at the Abbey. You moved and changed me.

To the employees of US Airways who lost our bags. I forgive you.

Doug, thanks for including me in the Abbey Program. Assuming you've read this far, you can see how much the experience meant to me. I will always be thankful and, as long as I can stand, I will stand with you. I love you.

Terry, I love you, man, and I thank God that I met you. I wonder if She's listening?

Thanks to all of my extended family. You have all had a tremendous impact on my life. I look forward to seeing you all and sharing our love at the MacIsland centennial 2015.

Mom, you inspired me to read and now write. I love you.

Dad, you are my hero. I love you.

Made in the USA
Lexington, KY
16 July 2014